OPEN UP OUR EYES

Moments That Shape Our Lives

Rabbi Charles A. Kroloff

BookLocker

Trenton, Georgia

Print ISBN: 979-8-88531-252-3
Ebook ISBN: 979-8-88531-253-0

Published by BookLocker.com, Inc., Trenton, Georgia.

Printed on acid-free paper.

BookLocker.com, Inc.
2022

First Edition

Library of Congress Cataloguing in Publication Data
Kroloff, Rabbi Charles A.
OPEN UP OUR EYES: Moments That Shape Our Lives by Rabbi Charles A. Kroloff
Library of Congress Control Number: 2022911814

DEDICATION

This volume is dedicated to
Our cherished grandchildren

Adam and Arielle
Jonathan and Aaron
Max, Ella, and Ben

I hope that my words will open their eyes to new horizons. But I know for certain that they have opened mine by their laughter, their kindness, their insights, and their love of life.

TABLE OF CONTENTS

INTRODUCTION

"Open up our eyes. Teach us how to live.

Fill our hearts with joy and all the love You have to give."

These words, from a song by Cantor Jeff Klepper, capture the theme of my book.

We all experience moments--over a lifetime--that bring into sharp focus what we value, what we prioritize, and what make us happy. These moments sharpen our vision and calibrate our moral compass. They help us adjust to the stark reality that we are flawed souls in an imperfect world. Most of all, they deepen our gratitude and leave us amazed.

Some of these moments impact us immediately; others have a delayed reaction. They lurk in the background of our psyches, waiting for us to reach back to them and only later to experience their wonder.

Memory triggers images and my mind's eye opens wider than before. I start to unearth new meaning from life experience. As I open my eyes to past wonders, I hope this will encourage you to travel a similar pathway and to uncover experiences that you may have forgotten altogether--or that you may have shunted aside. Some of them will now amaze you like they never did before. The cool thing about living is that it is never too late to open our eyes to the past, to discover new meaning in the present, to learn and to be amazed as we look to the future.

As we reflect on our past, present, and future, consider the words of Rabbi Abraham Joshua Heschel: "Our goal should be to live life in radical amazement...to get up in the morning and look at the world in a way that takes nothing for granted. Everything is phenomenal, everything is incredible. never treat life casually."

So let's get started. I invite you, the reader, to join me in recalling moments, small and large. As we turn them over in our minds, let's discover new insights that can guide us right now and into the future.

1. GROWING UP

The Buick Mascot

The 1946 Buick sported a hood ornament that caught the eyes of my friends and me as we played catch on the streets of Chicago's Southside. Its shiny metallic circle was clean, sleek, and so easily detachable that it frequently ended up on top of my friends' night tables.

One day, outside alone and with time on my hands, I decided to indulge in what seemed to my pre-adolescent mind as a relatively harmless act: the acquisition of an already very loose Buick mascot.

I didn't hide it. Rather, I proudly displayed it on my night table, exactly as my friends had done. That evening, the ornament caught my father's eye at which point he asked, "Where did this come from?"

Here's my explanation, almost verbatim: "It was pretty loose and about to fall off a nearby car. It was going to end up on the street anyway."

Decades later I still remember my father's words: "You'll have to return it first thing tomorrow."

"But why?" I asked, "everyone does it. I know at least six kids who did the very same thing."

Dad's response: "Six kids doing the wrong thing doesn't make it right. It's called stealing. You stole a piece of someone's car. Back it goes."

The next morning I found the owner, apologized, and offered to pay whatever it would cost to re-attach the ornament to the hood.

For that ten-year-old, it was one of the hardest days of his young life. For this octogenarian, looking back, it was one of the most important. Clearly, it was an early Eye Opener.

As a child, I thought that the most daring thing I could do was to steal that mascot, as my friends had done. But as Jim Hightower teaches, "The opposite of courage is not cowardice, it's conformity." In fact, the bravest thing I could have done was to do nothing at all. The Talmud makes this point on many occasions when it instructs: *"Shev v'al ta-aseh*. Sit and do nothing."

Years after my encounter with the Buick, as a rabbinic student, I studied Exodus: "Do not follow a multitude to do evil" (23.2).

There are some things we just do not do, even if lots of others do it. That youthful moment--embedded in my psyche--often pops up with red lights flashing. It happened one day when I picked up a NY Times at an airport news stand, had a plane to catch, and ten people were lined up to pay. Who would notice? I wouldn't be the first to rush back to a gate without plunking down the cash. Fortunately, the red lights flashed in my brain.

Or the time I learned of a breakthrough at a public company and thought--for a moment--about trading on information not available to others.

Many times in life, doing nothing is a courageous act. Perhaps it was your decision to stay far from a group intent on inflicting harm. Or to avoid an inebriated crowd. Or to stay off the road in dangerous conditions. When was it both right and wise for you to do nothing, rather than follow a crowd to do the wrong thing?

A Bugle

I was about nine when I joined the Cub Scouts. The group met a few blocks from our Chicago apartment, at the KAM Temple on Drexel Boulevard, across the street from what decades later would become the home of Barack and Michelle Obama. I learned to create a campfire by rubbing two stones together and to make enough lanyards to circle Chicago's Loop. I also joined the Drum & Bugle Corps. My parents bought me a dark brown, plastic (yes, plastic) bugle for $12, a hefty price those days that was probably equivalent to a week's groceries.

Five days after the purchase, I accidentally dropped the bugle, cracking it in two. I was devastated. I knew that the purchase was a sacrifice for my parents and I shuddered at the thought of their reaction. To this day, I remember how they received the news. "These things happen," they said, "We'll go back to the store this weekend and buy you another."

Instead of rebuke, understanding.
Instead of anger, compassion.
Instead of punishment, love.

Amelia Earhart taught, "A single act of kindness throws out roots in all directions, and the roots spring up and make new trees."

My parents' kind response to that broken bugle threw out roots of compassion that sprang up again and again during my lifetime. When one of our own children smashed a treasured item, that memory of my parents' measured response helped me muster the patience to defuse the moment.

Rabbi Jonathan Sacks, Chief Rabbi of Great Britain, taught: "Acts of kindness never die. They linger in the memory, giving life to other acts in return" (*From Optimism to Hope*, Bloomsbury, 2004).

Kindness spreads. If someone is kind and patient with me, that should inspire me to be patient with others. By the same token, if I am kind with myself, that should spur me to act with compassion toward others.

Those roots of kindness pop up when I am impatient with others. A single act of parental compassion, lingering in my memory, can act as a corrective reminding me to cool it. If my parents could instinctively forgive me for cracking that bugle, the least I can do is to be a more patient husband, father, teacher, friend, rabbi, or therapist. At times like that, I feel my father's presence with me in the moment. He lives on with me as I hope I will live on with my children, their children, and their children's children.

Think of this as a "chain reaction of kindness." Our parents' love instills in us a love for others who in turn reach out to their circle with compassion. And on and on it goes. Perhaps this is what we mean by immortality. This is one way that we, our parents, our children, our friends, all of us, live on.

In the *Amidah*, one of the central prayers in Jewish liturgy, we bless God "who remembers the love of our fathers and mothers." While this references the patriarchs and matriarchs (Abraham, Sarah, and other Biblical greats), I believe that God also remembers the love of our own parents, a love that becomes part of our spiritual and psychic narrative. As one of our prayers reminds us, "their love lives on in every act of goodness we perform and in the hearts of those who cherish their memory."

In what ways does the kindness of a parent live on with you? Think back on words they spoke or things they did that made you feel good about yourself and your future.

And what if your memory is not that of a loving parent? What if, growing up, you felt abused or emotionally abandoned? What if anger and impatience pervaded your home?

While this is not the youth I wish for anyone, there is a silver lining. I know more than a few who--with the help of therapy and/or religious insights--have navigated through the pain of parental neglect and have become the most caring and loving human beings on earth. Because of the pain of childhood, they were determined to live a different kind of life. And beyond your nuclear family, consider others in your life who supported you, blessed you, and left you with fond memories.

Aunts & Uncles:
More Important Than You Think

I was blessed with 16 uncles and aunts. Each one shaped my life, blessing me in ways that keep showing up in my daily life. As a kid, I thought everyone had 16. Today, I recognize this was an amazing gift.

Here's just one example. My mother's sister, Kate, and her husband, Abe, a highly respected plastic surgeon, welcomed me into their Long Island home over many summers. Every Wednesday, on my uncle's day off, we traveled with my cousins into Manhattan to take in a Broadway matinee. Mostly musicals, they opened my eyes to the wonders of the Broadway stage.

Seventy years later, those performances--their music and their star-studded casts--continue to amaze me: Oklahoma ("O What A Beautiful Morning"), Annie Get Your Gun ("There's No Business Like Show Business"), Carousel ("You'll Never Walk Alone"), South Pacific (Ezio Pinza and Mary Martin), and many more.

My life-long love affair with Broadway musicals-- especially the genius of Cole Porter, Lerner and Loewe, and Rodgers and Hammerstein--is a direct result of those matinees. As we packed into their car every Wednesday, did my aunt and uncle realize that they were instilling in their young nephew a passion for Broadway theater?

Perhaps. But what is clear to me now is that they--like every one of my aunts and uncles--made me feel as if I were a cherished part of their nuclear family. They differed from each other in terms of geography, resources, and educational backgrounds, but that was of little consequence. What was consequential was that each overflowed with love and affection, each cared about my unique self, and each enriched my life. They were--for a summer, a weekend, or for half a lifetime-- surrogate parents. Not to replace parents, but to augment. Not to compete with them, but to supplement. Not to by-pass them, but to complement them.

If you are blessed with aunts and uncles (great aunts and uncles count too), open your eyes to the blessings that they may have bestowed upon you. Consider the ways that they may still bless you now or tomorrow.

On the other hand, if you are blessed with nieces and nephews, think about how they might become a larger part of your life. And if you do not have uncles or aunts, nieces or nephews, extend your reach to cousins or family friends. Consider what gifts of friendship, counsel, or simple acts of love you might bestow upon them right now. Think about what a call, an email, or a work-related reference from you might mean to them. Here's the point: cherish those outside your immediate nuclear family. Consider them a unique extension of yourself with all the blessings that those relationships can yield.

2. JIM CROW SOUTH

Back of the Bus

Our family moved to Atlanta in 1946. World War II had just ended. Martin Luther King, Jr. was 17 years old and the "New South" was only a dream in the minds of a handful of progressive thinkers, like Ralph McGill, editor of the *Atlanta Constitution*, and like my Dad, Max N. Kroloff.

Jim Crow reigned supreme.

One summer, my naturally dark complexion turned even darker under Atlanta's searing summer sun. I boarded a bus to travel downtown. Taking an empty seat in the second row, I was promptly instructed by the driver: "Hey boy! You move to the back of the bus." I was too young and shocked to consider any alternative other than to follow his brusque order. I must have been so traumatized that I cannot remember ever sharing the incident with my parents.

Ten years later, my wife, Terry, and I flew from Cincinnati to New Orleans and then boarded a train to New Iberia, Louisiana where I would serve as the High Holyday student rabbi at Gates of Prayer synagogue. When the conductor collected our tickets, he told us we were not in the right seats and directed us to the car behind us, the last car, where we proceeded to move. It was only after sitting there for 30 minutes that Terry and I looked around and realized that everyone else was Black. The conductor had assumed that we were a mixed-race couple.

We didn't make a fuss. We had no objection to sitting in that car. I realize now that, had we resisted, we might have landed in a Louisiana jail...or worse. In 1890, the State of Louisiana enacted the Separate Car Act. Two years later Homer Plessy, a racially-mixed shoemaker, boarded a whites-only train car, aware that he would likely be arrested. His case eventually arrived at the U.S. Supreme Court that ruled--in its historic 7-1 decision in Plessy v. Ferguson-- that "separate but equal" is constitutional. Of course separate was never equal. (On January 5, 2022, nearly a century later, Gov. John Bel Edwards of Louisiana pardoned Plessy.)

Those two experiences--an Atlanta bus and a Louisiana train-- opened our eyes just a sliver to what it was like to be a Black American in the South. But for us, these were only momentary glimpses! The deprivation and terror that Blacks have endured are ten thousand times worse than anything we experienced.

We Jews are reminded--no, we are commanded--on Shabbat, at Passover, in the Books of Exodus, Leviticus and Deuteronomy to empathize with the stranger. Make sure that you treat everyone equally because, like you, the stranger is created in the image of God (Genesis 1.27). Never forget that you were an oppressed stranger in the land of Egypt (Exodus 23.9).

Rabbi Shai Held, Dean of Hadar Institute, teaches us that our Torah tradition could have responded differently to the experience of slavery. It could have argued that since we were oppressed and no one lifted a finger to help us, we have no obligation to empathize with or stand up for others. Instead, the Torah teaches us to "turn memory into empathy," to do justly and to create a more just society (website Hadar.com, *Parashat Mishpatim*).

Systemic Racism

I admired my Uncle Abe Goldstein who built a thriving business in Atlanta called Prior Tire Company. "Don't Cuss Call Us" was his firm's motto. But they not only fixed flats and pumped gas. In the rear of the building was a massive tire recapping operation: a dozen machines of all sizes--burning hot, smelly, and probably toxic-- where Black workers sealed fresh rubber onto thinly worn tires, giving them another 20 or 30 thousand miles of life. But they renewed not just tires for the family car; they recapped tires for mammoth earthmovers that the State of Georgia used to maintain roads and bridges.

As a kid, my eyes weren't focused on the dangerous working conditions that Black employees endured or on the strictly segregated tasks at every Atlanta business. My uncle was a very good man. I loved him dearly. He probably treated his workers better than most employers did. He did his best to live by the Jewish values he learned at the synagogue where he presided as president. He was advisor to every Atlanta mayor.

But Jim Crow lived everywhere.

As a kid in Georgia, I climbed Stone Mountain, a granite colossus-- bigger than Mount Rushmore--celebrating Robert E. Lee, Stonewall Jackson, and Jefferson Davis. I was frightened when the Ku Klux Klan held fiery vigils there, but that, like the mountain, was just part of the indelible Southern landscape that we accepted.

My encounters with racism were just that: encounters. They had a beginning and an end. They linger in my memory, but they do not define who I am from the moment I was born through every waking (and sleeping) hour thereafter. It was not until much later, spurred by the Black Lives Matter movement and informed by books like Isabel Wilkerson's *Caste*, Robin deAngelos' *White Fragility*, and Bryan Stevenson's *Just Mercy*, that my eyes began to open to the deeper meaning and implication of systemic racism in our nation.

It is now clear to me that all Americans must open their eyes to the 400 years of caste-based structural racism upon which we have shaped the American dream. And I must begin with myself, my privilege, my opportunities, my good fortune, much of which stand on the shoulders of a systemically oppressed people.

It feels strange to Jews and other groups--that have known unspeakable horrors--to grapple with two extremes: being both persecuted and entitled. The loss of six million Jews in the Holocaust is so overwhelming that the label of "white privilege" does not seem to make sense to us.

How is it possible that we Jews, persecuted through much of our history, can be labeled "privileged?" Do the educational, socio-economic, and human rights achievements of Jews in America somehow "balance" out the Holocaust, thereby rendering us privileged? They do not. This is not a sociological balancing act. It is simply a statement of fact: the privileges currently enjoyed by upper middle class white Americans were built on the backs of slavery, red lining, and very cheap labor.

Example: when I was growing up in Atlanta, nearly all my friends' families employed a domestic worker, usually full time. Most of my friends were not wealthy. Our family lived on a tight budget. "Maids", as they were called, were paid about one dollar a day in 1935. That's equivalent to $23 a day in 2021 dollars. At that pittance of a rate, households could "not afford" not to hire them.

I write this not to engage in a guilt trip, but to highlight that we continue to enjoy untold privileges at the expense of others. This was dramatically brought home to me in Tony Kushner's musical, "Caroline or Change," a play about the life of a Black domestic worker and her white Jewish employers in Louisiana who don't have a clue about what Caroline goes through every day of her weary life.

As I watched that play at the West Coast Black Theatre in Sarasota, Florida, my eyes opened wide. Memories rushed forth of our family's interaction with our housekeepers. I recalled one evening when, as a teenager, I arrived home half an hour late. As a result, our housekeeper missed her bus, waited a long hour for the next, and proceeded the next morning, to quit. Did I have a clue that I was adding misery to her misery?

As I struggle with what was then and what is now, I ask myself: Can we Jews, who know what it's like to be brutally oppressed, be a bridge across the racial divide? Are we capable of empathizing, building coalitions, and collaborating to achieve racial and economic justice? Are there enough of us who care and enough of us to make a difference?

Can we open our eyes to what happened to Black people in America since 1619, long before a single Jew stepped on this soil? As Rabbi Heschel taught, we are not all guilty, but we are all responsible. What has prevented us from seeing all this before now? Why has it taken so long? What's been going on in our own lives and attitudes that have blinded us to this reality? What changes are we prepared to make in how we see others and how we treat those who look different than we?

You've Got to be Carefully Taught

We're not born to hate. We're not born to see the world through the prism of skin color.

In 1949, Richard Rodgers captured this truth in the song, "You've Got to be Carefully Taught," written for the hit Broadway musical, South Pacific. Rodgers wrote that you've got to be taught "to hate and fear...from year to year." You have to be trained "to be afraid of people whose eyes are oddly made...or of people whose skin is a different shade." And that this teaching must come "before it's too late. Before you are six or seven or eight."

Eight years after Rodgers wrote these words, Terry and I directed a summer day camp in Jacksonville, Florida. One hot July day, we took the kids to the Jacksonville Zoo. My eyes nearly popped out of their sockets when I saw one of our six-year-old white campers patting the top of the hair of a Black kid he encountered on the zoo grounds. From the look on our camper's face, I surmised that he was trying to figure out just how different he was from this kid of color.

A few moments later I encountered two of our youngest campers standing in front of signs designating four (yes, four!) public bathrooms. They read: "White Men, White Women, Colored Boys, Colored Girls." Confused by the signage and trying to figure out his place in a caste system that adults strictly enforced, one turned to the other and innocently asked, "Are we white men?"

Years later, I relived those moments at the zoo when a White House photographer captured a much different, yet ironically reminiscent scene. In that iconic 2012 photo, President Barack Obama is bending over while 5-year old Jacob of Philadelphia, who is visiting the White House, strokes the hair of the President to see if it is like his. It is!

Lawrence Otis Graham was a widely read Black writer of the 1990s who grew up in the leafy suburban city of White Plains, New York. When he died, his obituary recalled how--as a ten year old--he was at a country club swimming pool with his brother and several white friends. But when he jumped in the water, his friends' parents quickly pulled them from the pool (*New York Times,* Mar. 5, 2021). That was 1971, three years after the assassination of Dr. Martin Luther King, Jr. and seven years after the passage of the historic Civil Rights Act of 1964.

"You've got to be carefully taught."

Growing up, I was "carefully taught" that God created us--every one of us--in God's own image (Genesis 1.26). In the Jim Crow South, that was Revolutionary! By my theological calculation that verse means that when white supremacists beat and lynched Black women, men, and children, they were beating and lynching souls precious to God! And when we close our eyes to the abject poverty that sends one out of every five American children to bed at night hungry, we are closing our eyes to the misery of God's children.

If the root causes of inequality are not dealt with, extremism from the right and left will grow. *Did you know that the United States has the widest economic chasm between "haves" and "have-nots" of any other nation on the planet?* Abject poverty produces unspeakable misery for God's children, many of whom live just a few miles from us.

But proximity also presents opportunity. In 2000, my close friend Warren Eisenberg (co-founder of BedBath&Beyond) invited me to join him in an effort to provide educational opportunities to children of low-income families. With the support of Warren and the collaboration of Temple Emanu-El of Westfield (NJ), we launched "I Have A Dream-Plainfield."

Some background: In 1986, Eugene Lang returned to the East Harlem (NY) school from which he had graduated a half century prior to deliver the sixth grade commencement address. He looked out at the kids, scrapped his prepared remarks, and told them that one of his most memorable moments was hearing Dr. King, deliver his "I Have A Dream" speech in 1963 and that every one should have a dream. In Lang's words, "Then I decided to tell them I'd give a scholarship to every member of the class admitted to a four-year college."

Inspired by Lang and the programs that he spawned, we promised a cohort of 53 first-graders at Plainfield's Clinton School that--if they completed high school--we would cover the equivalent of four-years of state college tuition. For 18 years, our team of volunteers and one professional supported our "Dreamers" with tutoring, counseling, cultural enrichment, and mentoring. The result was, as one student said, "I start to think of college and the rest of life in a new way." Ninety-four percent of our Dreamers completed high school or its equivalent and nearly all of those went on to post-secondary education with some attaining Masters degrees. In contrast, less than 70% of Plainfield students were graduating high school in that era.

No matter where you reside, you will find opportunities to mentor, counsel, tutor, and support. Perhaps you are already doing something to help a student move ahead and, if so, please share your experiences with family, friends, and co-workers. Let them know what can happen if we all pull together to help kids realize their dreams.

"You've got to be carefully taught."

(There are also rewards for you. The most important one, of course, is that you are helping to save a life. In addition, a recent Harvard University study revealed that "older adults who volunteer 100 hours or more per year reduce their chance of early death and boost levels of optimism and purpose in life than those who did not volunteer as much or not at all" (*Chicago Tribune*, July 9, 2022).

3. BUILDING CONFIDENCE

Taking On Responsibility

Growing up, I was not a "three-sport athlete." Not even one sport. I loved baseball, but inevitably was the last to be chosen for the pick-up game. I was usually assigned to patrol deep right field, waiting under the brutal Georgia sun for what seemed like hours until a ball came my way.

I was shorter than most of my friends and when my parents took me to a department store for my bar mitzvah suit, we ended up in the section labeled "Chubby." I dreaded swimming. When I entered a pool, I seemed to go straight to the bottom.

But thanks to loving parents, insightful teachers, a rabbi (Jacob M. Rothschild) who encouraged me at every Jewish turn, and a Zionist youth organization that offered me leadership opportunities, my confidence grew to the point where I developed a pretty good sense of self.

In Atlanta, I worked for a few weeks over several summers at Prior Tire Co. My Uncle Abe gave me more responsibility than a 12-year-old kid could ever imagine. Not only did I pump gas, but I oversaw the entire station when the manager took lunch or was on vacation.

On occasion, I was in charge of Abe's parking lot adjacent to a medical building where, barely able to see above the dashboard, I maneuvered cars into narrow slots. That was two years before I was eligible for a Georgia driver's permit (age 14 in the 1940s).

Today, I observe many children growing up with an abundance of privileges and a scarcity of responsibilities. Parents helicopter into every aspect of their children's lives to defend, protect, and advocate. A few illegally hire surrogates to take entrance exams for their kids. The clear message: "You can't do this; I'll do it for you."

As a rabbi, I regularly met with 12-year-olds prior to bar or bat mitzvah to discuss their approaching *simcha* (celebration). At some sessions, parents would accompany them. Looking directly into the eyes of the student, I would ask the child a question. Sometimes, before the youngster could utter a single word, the parent would respond for the child. What a shame, I thought, this student has a mind and a voice, but her parent won't let her shine forth.

Did You Ask Any Good Questions Today?

Just as important as letting kids figure out their own answers is encouraging them to ask good questions.

The ability of children to ask questions is a powerful tool in cognitive development. As kids question, they are gathering information they need in order to learn about the world and solve problems. When children start school, those from households that encourage curiosity have an edge over the rest of their classmates. Practice in taking in information from their parents leads to acquiring information from their teacher. In other words, they know how to learn better and faster (Michael M. Chouinard, Monograph 12936, National Library of Medicine).

My father loved to tell the story of Nobel Prize physicist Isidor Rabi. Dr. Rabi was once asked: "Why do you think you have become such a successful scientist?" His response: "Every day when I came home from school, my mother didn't inquire if I gave the right answers. Instead, she greeted me with this: "Did you ask your teachers any good questions today?"

Questions and answers are the lifeblood of the Talmud. It's the way Jews have learned for 2,000 years. Curiosity breeds learning and learning builds 1) independence, 2) confidence, and 3) a better life.

Independence strengthens confidence. When I was nine, my mother sent me on a streetcar downtown to Chicago's Loop with a Marshall Field & Co. charge card to purchase a few shirts. When I handed the clerk the card, she insisted that I bring my mother to the counter. It took me five minutes to convince the sales person that I had come by myself.

While I might not recommend such a juvenile foray to Chicago's Loop today, in those simpler times, it taught me that I could do more than I ever thought possible. Parents need to take reasonable risks as they give their kids freedom to explore, experiment, and exercise independence. The confidence gained is priceless.

What have been the most important confidence-building experiences in your life so far? What have you done lately to gain more confidence? As you interact with co-workers, family, students, or even friends, what steps have you taken to help them build self-confidence?

Expect More of Yourself

I arrived at Yale when I was 16. (Not recommended, but there I was.) After registering and picking up my library card, my next requirement was to show up at Yale's iconic 14-story, gothic-style Payne Whitney Gymnasium to take the "freshman swim test."

The required test consisted of swimming four lengths of the 25-yard pool without stopping, a feat I had never even once performed. With trepidation (would I have to leave Yale if I didn't pass?), I managed to complete the task, but just barely. Decades later, I still remember the instructor's words: "Well, Kroloff, technically, you passed the test. But I strongly suggest that you take the swimming course this semester."

I did exactly that and will be forever grateful to the instructor for some of the best advice I ever received. To my great surprise, swimming has become one of my favorite pastimes. The kid who could barely swim four lengths, as an octogenarian now does a whole lot more than that.

Not all of Yale's requirements that orientation week were benign. From the 1940s through the 70s, 16 universities, including most of the Ivies and the Seven Sisters took nude posture photos of incoming students. Ostensibly taken to gauge the rate of skeletal deformity in the population, they were likely used to support racist eugenic theories. The concept was later debunked and the photos transferred to the Smithsonian Institution where most were destroyed. The comedian Dick Cavett--we overlapped one year at Yale--called it "officially sanctioned soft-porn." It is amazing that school authorities permitted the practice and that none of us or our parents thought to object.

From these experiences I have learned two valuable--though seemingly contradictory--lessons, both found in *Pirke Avot*, the Ethics of the Fathers. In *Avot* 2.3, Rabban Gamaliel taught: "Be heedful of the ruling power, for they bring no person nigh to them except for their own need. They seem to be friends at such time as it is to their benefit, but they do not stand by a person when he is in need."

Yet, in the next Chapter, Rabbi Hanina said: "Pray for the welfare of the ruling power, since, but for fear of it, men would have swallowed up each other alive" (3.2).

I shall be forever grateful to the "swim authorities" who may have saved my life and forever be repelled by the "posture authorities" who took advantage of a half million young women and men.

I welcome strong political leadership on a local and national level. I applaud the pro-active initiatives of Westfield's mayor, Shelley Brindle's, to renew Westfield's downtown, our Congressman Tom Malinowski's defense of human rights, and President Biden's efforts to strengthen the social safety net and renew America's infrastructure. At the same time, I am angry when government lies to me (e.g. *Pentagon Papers* on the war in Vietnam or the false narrative justifying our invasion of Iraq). While both political parties share responsibility for these disasters, in recent times leaders of the Republican party have dangerously defended the Big Lie and continue to undermine the foundations of our democracy. They are literally placing in grave jeopardy the future of our Republic.

Two take aways: One, local politics and civic responsibility are the building blocks of good government. Enlightened, progressive leaders who care more about community than personal power or self-aggrandizement can do wonders. Citizen leaders must model a system where mediation, compromise, and good faith negotiation are the coin of the realm. I urge you to become active in local government or public service organizations that make our world a better place, community by community.

Second, a healthy two party system provides the checks and balances required for building a just and peaceful society. We must hold our representatives accountable and insist that they denounce the polarizing forces that are tearing our nation apart.

4. TAKING RISKS

College at Sixteen

I am inherently risk-adverse. When I contemplate a trip, I think of ten things that can go wrong. When the Covid19 pandemic engulfed us, I ventured forth as little as possible (probably a wise idea).

When I was a junior at Henry Grady High School in Atlanta, the Ford Foundation came calling. With the Korean War raging, educators sought to push high-performing students through college so that they could complete their studies before being called to war. Four universities--Yale, Wisconsin, Columbia and Chicago—each agreed to reserve 50 places in their Class of 1955 so long as the student would be 16 1/2 or younger at matriculation. Ford was also interested in learning whether early admission to college was educationally desirable.

On recommendation of my principal and with the appealing offer of SATs without a fee, I applied. Off I went to Israel that summer with little expectation of anything other than completing senior year at Grady.

In early July, I received a static-filled transatlantic telephone call from my parents announcing that I had been accepted at Yale--my first and only choice--with full tuition scholarship. "No pressure," my parents said, "but Yale needs your response in 24 hours. It's non-deferrable, and your principal thinks you should go for it."

I went for it, unsuspecting that, as a naive public high school boy recovering from nasal surgery, I would be tossed into classes and social scenes with young men two years my senior. More than half of my freshman class had been preparing for Yale since the day they were born, most recently at elite prep schools such as Hotchkiss, Exeter, and Andover.

The Ford Foundation concluded, years later, that early admission, while educationally appealing, presented emotional challenges for 16-year-olds that were difficult to surmount. I often felt like an outlier, but the academic opportunities were exhilarating.

Risk/Reward.

When faced with big-time decisions, I try to do a risk/reward analysis. In retrospect, while the challenge of social maladjustment loomed, the opportunity to study with extraordinary professors and engage in expansive extra-curricular experiences like the varsity debate team and Hillel made it worthwhile. Full tuition scholarship was appealing. On balance, I probably made the right decision.

When you make a decision for the right reasons, it usually works out well. Not always, but right reasons give you a big leg up. For example, when faced with the opportunity to move to another job and/or another city, what are the pros and cons that you should consider? While financial reward is important, what values should come into play? Family? Personal wellness? Cultural opportunities? Access to your faith community? If you identify your values and priorities--the ground of your authentic self--and base your decision on them, there is a high likelihood that you will make a decision that is right for you and those dear to you.

What has been your experience with risk/reward? Think of three high-risk decisions that you have made over the years. How often did you take the risk? What values did you take into account? How did each risky venture work out?

Consider the times you declined the risk and stayed put. How do you feel about those decisions? There's no correct answer, no one-size-fits-all, but I'll wager that--if your decisions were driven by your values--you feel good about most of them, whether they were "go for it" or stand pat.

Making the Choice Right

Each of us has his or her own tolerance for risk. But in nearly every case, we have the ability to make whatever decision we take, the right one.

My colleague, Rabbi Norman Hirsh, taught couples in pre-marital discussion that "falling in love is making the <u>right choice</u>. Building our love is making the <u>choice right</u>." So it is with much of life. Most of the time, it is up to us to make whatever choice we have made "the right choice." And if, after trying hard, that seems impossible, then we must acknowledge our mistake and move on.

Terry and I took another risk when we left the bucolic confines of Hebrew Union College (HUC) in Cincinnati to study for a year in Israel. Most of my professors thought this was a terrible, perhaps even career-shattering, decision. "We have more to teach you here in Cincinnati," they insisted, "than you can ever acquire in Israel."

But Terry and I grew up in the Zionist youth organization, Young Judea, which made us lovers of Israel to the core. We were inspired by the example of our dear friends and fellow rabbinic student Bob Samuels and his wife, Annette, who were completing two years in Israel as we headed there. A few years later, they made *aliyah* (settling in Israel) where Bob transformed the Leo Baeck School in Haifa into an educational colossus of pluralism and academic achievement.

If you are risk-adverse, it helps to have mentors like the Samuels who show us how to do it.

It's also advantageous to be married to a woman who is ready to go for anything that will expand her horizons. Buoyed by our dreams, we embarked on the Cunard Line's Queen Mary for a year of study in Israel. The Jewish State was then ten years old!

Looking back, this is what I learned: when you have a once-in-a-lifetime opportunity to break out of the routine-way of doing things, and when you suspect that the rewards might be life-transforming, go for it!

In 1969, Jews in the Soviet Republic of Georgia petitioned for the right to emigrate to Israel. The news sent shock waves throughout Soviet Zionist circles and the worldwide Jewish community. It put the lie to the Soviet myth that their Jewish citizens were happy and felt no connection to Israel. It was a dangerous act that placed the petition signers at risk of long jail terms.

As the movement grew, tens of thousands of Soviet Jews appealed for exit visas. Nearly all were refused, hence the term "refusenik." Many were jailed and some exiled to far-off provinces. The most well known refusenik was Natan Sharansky who spent 12 years in Soviet prisons, much of it in solitary confinement or hard labor.

In the 1970s, courageous American Jews (including members of our synagogue) embarked on "secret" missions to the USSR to support refuseniks. In 1982, Terry and I were invited to undertake a surreptitious trip to bring medicines, religious materials, and kosher food to Jews who not only were denied exit visas, but who also lost their employment because they criticized the regime.

Along with Freda and Leonard Posnock, we spent months preparing for the trip. Leonard, the owner of *Shofar* kosher food products, assembled an assortment of bologna, salami, and hot dogs, all in plain wrappers without the *Shofar* label. With our suitcases lined with "Jewish contraband," we flew off to Moscow. Changing planes at Helsinki, we flushed away, in the airport's toilets, the notes we had memorized: names, addresses and telephone contacts of refuseniks.

We visited dozens of refuseniks and were dazzled by their courage, resilience, and humor. Humor? On the fun-filled holiday of Purim, we joined a dozen refusenik families for a clandestine Purim party, a high-risk venture in the anti-Jewish USSR. Two KGB secret police in black trench coats, who had followed us on the subway, posted themselves at the entrance of the apartment building.

We ascended three flights to join the festivities. After an hour of singing and dancing, we heard banging on the front door. Terry and I looked at each other as our hearts dropped to our toes, certain that we were goners. How many years in a Soviet prison? The intruders burst in yelling, *Chag Sameach,*" Happy Holiday. They were fellow refuseniks intent on playing a big joke on all of us.

We had never met Jews who were willing to risk all in order to live free Jewish lives. We had never met women and men who had the strength to play practical jokes on themselves (and us) while KGB kept watch downstairs.

5. FINDING JOY EVERY DAY

Those fun-loving refuseniks were fulfilling the dictum of the wise Chasidic teacher, Rabbi Nachman of Bratslav, "It is a *mitzvah* (commandment) to go about joyfully in the world" (Likutey Moharan II, 24).

Each of us faces challenges. They may involve health, finances, employment, or family. The Covid pandemic pushed many of us to the breaking point. Losses mounted and strength drained from us. Marital discord mushroomed and financial stress grew. Students were strained to the extreme while front-line health care workers felt abandoned. We questioned the meaning of it all.

Rabbi Nachman reminds us that every day we are obligated to discover joy in the world. Here are some steps we can take to find daily joy:

Discover beauty and peace in nature.

Have a good conversation with children, grandchildren, relatives, or friends (virtually or in person).

Enjoy five minutes in front of a great work of art.

Listen to music that touches your soul.

Study a text that might enrich your spirit.

Taste a new food to excite your palate.

Enjoy a warm shower.

Take an energetic swim

Go for a calming walk.

Say a prayer.

Where do you find your daily dose of joy? Do you know that--when you smile--you release endorphins? Endorphins are neurotransmitters triggered by the movements of the muscles in your face. They make us feel happy and lower our stress levels.

Surprisingly, endorphins work whether you fake a smile or whether it's the real thing. (They also work with laughter.) They function as a painkiller. People who suffer from chronic pain discover that a good laugh is often an effective antidote.

Norman Cousins opened my eyes to the importance of laughter. A political journalist, UCLA professor, and editor of the *Saturday Review*, Cousins was diagnosed in 1964 with a painful degenerative illness which traditional medicine was unable to treat. During extended periods in the hospital and at home, Cousins ordered Marx Brothers films and reruns of Candid Camera. Watching those iconic routines, Cousins laughed himself into better health.

He shared his experience in his best-selling *Anatomy of An Illness as Perceived by the Patient: Reflections on Healing and Regeneration* (W. W. Norton 1979). An early advocate of a humanistic approach to medical care, Cousins was a forerunner of mindfulness and meditation. Those practices help us stay in the moment, reduce stress, and improve sleep.

Though he died in 1990, Cousins continues to open my eyes. When I am feeling low, I often force myself to smile and, within seconds, my spirit rises. No charge. No doctor's prescription. This addiction--to smiles or laughter--is good for your health.

6. THE AMAZING JOY OF SHABBAT

During the worst days of the Covid-19 epidemic, several people said to me, "Everyday is Wednesday," meaning, of course, that every day is just like every other. I instinctively, but gently responded, "Not if you celebrate Shabbat."

Rabbi Heschel helps us to understand the beauty of Shabbat, especially through his brief, spiritually exhilarating book, *The Sabbath* (Noonday Press, 1975). Heschel teaches that the purpose of the Sabbath is to celebrate time rather than space. For six days a week we llve under the tyranny of things. We're busy trying to dominate the world. That all changes on Shabbat when we try to dominate the self and become attuned to holiness in time.

Shabbat not only helped me maintain my spiritual balance as Covid-19 raged, it has brought me blessings every week for most of my life. I did not grow up in a Shabbat-observant home. Terry and I discovered the power of Shabbat during our year in Israel. Stores closed Friday by three pm. Jerusalem traffic came to a halt as Shabbat prayers echoed through ancient alleyways and in the nascent Reform synagogue that we attended. On Saturday afternoon, we dared not call friends between two and four because that was the time for their Shabbat nap.

We brought our passion for Shabbat back home with us. It's not easy for rabbis with a congregation to enjoy a leisurely Friday evening meal with family, but we were determined to always be together for candles, *kiddush* over wine, *motzi* over challah, Shabbat dinner, *birkat hamazon* (blessing after our meal), and *z'mirot* (songs). According to tradition, the glow of Shabbat remains through Tuesday when anticipation of the next Shabbat starts anew. Saturday afternoon was "holy time" in our family. We hiked, played tennis, swam, biked, read together, and socialized with other families. I resisted requests for synagogue programing on Saturday afternoon because Shabbat with family was indispensible to our spiritual health.

That was *our* Shabbat, but there is no single way to observe Shabbat. Some Orthodox Jews endeavor to follow *halacha*, Jewish law, by refraining from all forms of "work." When defined strictly that means not riding in a car or turning on any form of electricity. For Reform Jews, it can mean any of the following: a special Shabbat dinner preferably at home with appropriate blessings, family togetherness, prayer, Torah study, recreation, personal renewal, and rest.

Heschel describes Shabbat as our "cathedral of time." I try to live in that holiness of time by not opening my computer on Shabbat, not paying bills or changing light bulbs, and staying out of grocery stores. But I'll buy a frozen yogurt for a Shabbat delight and use my cell phone, but only as little as possible). On some *Shabbatot* (plural for Shabbat), Terry and I head for the hills, that is, for a cool walking trail accompanied, when possible, by family.

I cannot imagine what my life would be without Shabbat once every seven days. You don't have to be Jewish to love Shabbat and, if you're not Jewish, it just might be Sunday. If your work schedule requires it, your Shabbat could occur on one of the other five days of the week. For Jews, the fact that our community recognizes Friday night and Saturday as Shabbat creates a powerful sense of spiritual togetherness. The fact that other Jews in my community and around the world observe Shabbat on Saturday has a powerful impact on me. But for non-Jews, the joy and renewal of Shabbat can occur any day.

7.   WHAT TRAGIC LOSS CAN TEACH US

My father died suddenly at age 51. He barbecued dinner for friends on July 3. Early the next morning, the Fourth of July, he suffered a coronary occlusion and died almost immediately.

Terry and I were traveling in Europe, returning from our year in Israel. Because of an accident with our car that threw us off schedule, our family could not reach us. After waiting several days, they had no choice but to proceed with the funeral without us.

God's Repair People

We missed the first few days of *shiva* (the traditional seven days of mourning after the funeral). On our arrival at my parents' Maryland residence, we were embraced by family who had gathered and remained until our return. Their presence was step one on our pathway to healing.

The visit of one rabbi, Balfour Brickner, made a lasting impression on me. I had met with Balfour years before, but he did not know us well (our family belonged to a different Washington, DC synagogue). He drove 45 minutes to see us, spent an unrushed hour, and consoled us in a manner that I vividly recall decades later.

The next time you ponder whether or not to call or visit someone who has suffered a loss, ponder less and act more. Your words can be few, but your presence delivers a dose of compassion that can bring a lifetime of healing.

In the Talmud, Rabbi Hama teaches that when we comfort the mourner, we are "walking in God's way" (Babylonian Talmud, *Sotah,*14a). When we walk in God's way, we are serving as God's helpers.

Keep your eyes focused on this: we are mere mortals, imperfect and limited, mere specks in an unfathomable universe. And yet, imagine this: we who are specks can be God's assistants. Consider yourself God's "Repair People." If that isn't a privilege, I don't know what is.

A few years ago, I delivered an opening blessing at the annual breakfast of IMAGINE, an exceptional Westfield area agency that offers free year-round grief support for children, families, and communities. Many of their clients are young children who recently lost a parent.

I began by saying, "It is clear that God did not create a perfect world. This world we live in is full of imperfection, failings, disappointments, and tragedy. Most of the imperfections are not due to any fault of ours. Nor do we have a good explanation for the sad events that often overwhelm us.

"When Rabbi Harold Kushner wrote his best seller, he did not title it: '<u>WHY Bad Things Happen to Good People</u>.' Instead, he called it: '*WHEN Bad Things Happen to Good People*.' He did not try to explain why tragedy occurs. Instead, he taught us how to listen, how to empathize, how to engage, and how to guide those who have suffered loss onto a pathway of healing.

"I believe that God has sent us into this imperfect world to be God's 'Repair People.' We are here to lift up the fallen, to free the oppressed, to heal the sick, to support those wounded in body and soul. IMAGINE is part of God's repair team."

The rabbinic sages put it this way:
> The wheat is to be ground.
> The seeds are to be soaked.
> And the human being is to be repaired.
> (*Tanchuma, Bereshit* 11.6)

In Hebrew, we call this effort: *tikun olam*, repairing the world. There is no calling higher than to be one of God's Repair People.

When the patriarch Abraham was convalescing, three visitors arrived to comfort him (Genesis, Ch.18). In Hebrew, these visitors are called *malachim*, or messengers. Commentators suggest that the three were like angels who were representing God. When we visit the sick, we are God's messengers, bringing repair and hope.

Facing Mortality

As I began to deal with the shocking news of my father's sudden death, one of the first things I, at 24 years, thought about was my own mortality. Death has a way of forcing you to consider life in ways you never have before. I was a year short of rabbinic ordination, with the expectation that I would soon be comforting others. Did that mean that I was better prepared than others to deal with this tragic loss? Not a chance!

You may be a physician, nurse, or therapist. No matter what you do for a living, you're probably no better prepared to deal with death than the average person.

Serious illness and death compel us to think about subjects that we prefer to avoid: Our life is finite, we never know what is around the corner. In the larger scheme of things, some of our priorities are badly screwed up.

Be Careful What You Wish For

Leo Tolstoy's story of a peasant named Pahom was an Eye Opener for me. Pahom was offered the "deal of a lifetime." For a thousand rubles, he could walk around as large an area as he wished from daybreak to sunset. All the territory he covered will be his so long as he returns to the starting point by sunset. If not, he will forfeit the land he covered and the rubles.

Pahom is thrilled as he sets out--traveling as far as he can--until he suddenly realizes that he has gone so far that he may not be able to return to the starting point by sunset. He turns and races back as quickly as possible. Arriving at the starting point just as the sun is setting, he is so exhausted that he collapses and dies.

Tolstoy titles his eye-opening story, "How Much Land Does A Man Need?" The answer: We need less land and more wellness of body and soul.

8. SELF CARE IS A GAME CHANGER

I expected my 51st birthday to be my most difficult. Twenty years before that milestone, I anticipated all kinds of terrible things happening to me, mainly cardiovascular. I recall the frightening eye opener that my internist and dear friend, Sandy Reiss, offered me when I approached my forties: "Chuck, it's 95 percent your genes and five percent in your control."

It was then that I literally took the plunge. I made the pool at our local Y my second home. At first, I didn't cover much more than the four laps that I managed at my Yale freshman swim test. Gradually, I built up to 36 figuring "double *chai*" couldn't hurt. (*Chai* means life. Hebrew letters have a numerical equivalent. The two letters in *chai* equal 18. Double is 36.) Three days a week I would leave my study before noon so that I could be showered and dressed in time for one of my frequent lunch meetings.

When that 51st year came around, it wasn't as scary as I anticipated because I had made some lifestyle decisions that left me feeling better about myself, physically and spiritually. Dr. Reiss's five percent was not encouraging, but since those were the cards I had been dealt, I had better use that meager percentage to my advantage.

Years later, I learned that the odds are much better than my doctor observed. As reported by Dr. Sanjay Gupta, "Our everyday experiences, including what we eat, how much we exercise, with whom we socialize, what challenges we face, how well we sleep, and what we do to reduce stress and learn, factor much more into our brain health and overall wellness than we can imagine" (*Keep Sharp*, New York, Simon & Schuster, 2021, pp. 13-14).

According to Gupta, a study in *Neuroscience Research* and published in the journal *Genetics* revealed that whom we marry has a greater influence on how long we live than our genetic inheritance does. Surprisingly, the researchers concluded that genes account for less than seven percent of our lifespan.

When I was nominated to become president of the Central Conference of American Rabbis (CCAR), the worldwide association of Reform rabbis. I conferred with a few cherished colleagues as I tried to identify what would be the cornerstone of my tenure. Rabbi Marc Disick asked, "What is the greatest gift you can give to your colleagues?" Without hesitation, I responded: "A pathway to wellness." Our first task was to ask rabbis to open their eyes to this harsh reality: we clergy are so busy taking care of others that we do not pay attention to our own self care.

I had observed dozens of rabbis going off the rails because they did not take care of themselves. Nor was I myself exempt from this, having struggled with self-neglect from time to time in my rabbinate.

Clergy fall victim to two fatal fallacies. First, that taking care of others is equivalent to taking care of oneself. The fallacy works this way. We become rabbis because we are natural caregivers. We get pleasure from helping others. (We joke that we are paid to do what we love doing.) So it's natural to conclude that the personal fulfillment we get from doing our job and the compliments we receive from taking care of our congregants or community is all we need to stay healthy and productive.

Of course, it doesn't work that way. Being a rabbi is draining. Unless we replenish our resources, slow down our rabbinic motor, and pay attention to the needs of our own body and spirit, we will eventually fall apart. The same is true of other professions, such as physician, dentist, therapist, police officer, or teacher, to mention but a few. What other lines of work drain body or soul?

The second fallacy is that, if we take good care of others, then others will take good care of us. True, others do care about us--spouses, children, some of the leaders with whom we work. But at the end of the day, the "wellness buck" stops with us. If we don't care about ourselves, what others may do for us will have little impact.

Rabbis (like many others) work very hard. On weekends, when our family and friends have time off, we are on. Rabbi Jack Stern, Jr., who led Temple Emanu-El for six years, once said: "We rabbis teach the importance of Shabbat, yet we are the first to get up from the Shabbat table and rush off to lead the service." We respond to calls at two a.m. and race to a home where a 62-year-old suddenly died or to the intensive care unit after a motorcycle accident.

We hope that our temple officers will recognize the stress that we deal with, that they will ask how we are doing, and will "take care of us" as we take care of them. Sometimes it happens that way--and I am grateful to all who have inquired about my wellbeing and that of my colleagues. But it does not occur often. Ultimately, we must take care of ourselves. Few people ever asked me if I was getting enough rest, had enough time for my family, or whether I was able to grab a free Shabbat. Few inquired if our clergy team or our staff receives the support we need to do our jobs and stay healthy.

I compare self-care to the instructions we receive from a flight attendant before takeoff: "In the event of loss of cabin air pressure, oxygen masks will drop from the compartment above. Before helping a child or others, place the mask on your face first."

We in the helping professions are often described as "wounded healers." What sustains us also depletes us. Consider placing Rabbi Hillel's teaching on your desk or night table:

If I am not for myself, who will be for me?
But if I am only for myself, who am I?
And if not now, when?
(*Ethics of the Fathers*, 1.14)

What steps do you take to care for yourself? Do you have mentors you turn to, a peer group that enriches you, a therapist who listens to you, a good friend who is honest with you? I have never met a single person --and I don't think there is one--who does not need a trusted friend or mentor.

Therapy. Who Me?

I trained as a marital and family therapist at the Institutes for Religion and Health in New York City. One of the requirements for certification was to engage in our own personal therapy. It should be clear that a therapist (or clergyperson) is ill equipped to assist others unless she has worked through many of her own issues through personal psychotherapy.

I was expected to provide my supervisor with the name of my therapist by November of my first semester. That date came and went. Early February, my supervisor informed me: "Chuck, you have one week to make that arrangement or you will be dropped from the program." Within 48 hours she had the name.

Why did I drag my feet? Why did I put off establishing a therapeutic relationship? During my undergraduate years, I had met short-term with a therapist at the Yale Health Center to deal with the stress of undergraduate life. But this was different. How long will I be in therapy? What will it cost? What will I look like at the other end?

I was afraid of what I might discover about myself. I feared what another person--in this case a trained professional--would learn about me. I felt vulnerable. Perhaps I was not as strong as I pretended to be. I was reluctant to face changes that I might have to undertake. What would I learn about my marriage, my relationship to our children, my feelings about my parents and sister, my competitive spirit, my sexuality, and my masculinity? Men are 40 percent less likely than women to pursue counseling. Some of us need a push.

I considered myself a rather successful rabbi. Would I change in ways that would make me less effective in my rabbinic role? It took me months to get comfortable with the therapeutic process, but ultimately it may have saved me from going down paths that I might regret. I continued in therapy well beyond the twelve months that my training program required. I reflect on it almost weekly although my last session was decades ago.

I have long urged that every rabbinic and cantorial student at HUC be required to undertake personal psychotherapy. Before we can help others, we clergy must have a better understanding of ourselves. Every faculty or administrator at HUC with whom I have conferred has agreed. Therapy is now available to many rabbinic and cantorial students. I look forward to the time when it will be a requirement.

Indeed, everyone engaged in a helping profession would benefit from personal therapy. We all have unresolved issues that we need to come to terms with. Society benefits when we are able to work through those issues with a therapist or counselor rather than acting them out through behavior that can be destructive and harmful to those we serve.

To its credit, the CCAR, which represents thousands of Reform rabbis, now offers an extensive menu of wellness programs including workshops that address clergy burnout, the stress of serving small, under staffed congregations, and the tensions inherent in clergy reviews. While these seminars are highly effective, they are no substitute for personal therapy.

How many times in your life have you felt that you would like to turn to a counselor or therapist? What are the issues you would like to deal with and what are the obstacles standing in the way of making the move? If you're feeling blocked, have a conversation with a professional--perhaps your physician, minister, rabbi, or priest--and explore the possibility.

9. SURPRISE! LOOK WHO'S RESILIENT

Each year, I deliver a talk prior to the Yizkor (Memorial) Service on Yom Kippur. In 2020, the Holydays occurred while the Coronavirus pandemic raged out of control

That year, I encouraged our congregants to think about lessons they learned, from friends, family or others, that might help them navigate two great challenges we were confronting: the virulent coronavirus and the brutally polarized political landscape of our nation. As I was composing my message, I had an Eye Opener of my own. To my amazement, my focus pivoted to my mother who lived to age 95.

That surprised me because it was my father, not my mother, who had been the dominant influence in my formative years. Or so I thought. When my father died, we wondered how my mother would manage. She was the youngest of eight children; her mother died when she was five. As I was growing up, she had a few ailments and seemed dependent upon my father.

When he died, my mother reinvented herself. She transitioned from a dependent soul to a no-nonsense, pragmatic woman who knew how to get things done for herself and others. At age 87, she relocated from Washington, DC to Westfield where she demonstrated, again and again, her ability to adapt to new circumstances. She became the go-to-person for her senior neighbors who needed assistance in navigating the vagaries of Medicare and Medicaid. She invested her limited funds like a pro in high yield CDs and conservative equities.

My mother demonstrated a resilience that I never realized she had. Resilience is the capacity to recover quickly from difficulties and to exhibit toughness as needed. That resilience was reflected in her take-charge attitude. When I offered to do something for her, she often surprised me by responding, "I can do that."

Her persistence reinforced her resilience. She was not deterred if a store clerk refused to do her bidding. "Let me talk to your manager" was her response and that got results. Her resilience was demonstrated in her street smarts. She was alert to scams, conscious of price, and aware of her surroundings. Not a bad formula for an aging senior living independently. While I appreciated some of this resilience during her lifetime, it wasn't until years after her death that I fully grasped how resilient she was.

I offer this example not to engage in nostalgia (though I confess that I do enjoy it), but to encourage you to think of people in your life who are stronger and more resilient than you realized. Consider friends or family who, as they responded to loss, rose to the occasion and unleashed hidden skills that enabled them not merely to survive, but to enjoy life

Not until we are tested do we discover who we are and what we can do. Before scientists were faced with the Coronavirus pandemic, it seemed impossible that a vaccine could be developed, tested, and approved in less than 12 months. But confronted with the greatest worldwide health crisis in a century, they accomplished the inconceivable.

We Are Strong at the Broken Places

Ernest Hemingway wrote: "The world breaks everyone and afterward many are strong at the broken places" (*A Farewell to Arms*).

I have a friend, let's call her Ruth, whose 12-year-old daughter was killed while riding her bicycle. Shortly afterward, Ruth contracted cancer and, in order to save her life, her leg was amputated above the knee. Yet, with each challenge, my friend grew not weaker, but more resilient and strong at the broken place.

Her resilience came from three insights:

First, although she loved her daughter dearly and would have done anything in the world to save her, Ruth's daughter was *part* of her life, not *all* of her life. Same for her leg. It was a pivotal part of her body, but not all of it, and she learned to function well with her prosthesis.

I visited Ruth in the hospital the day after surgery. We spoke about the operation and somehow I stumbled into asking her how she was handling yet another loss. I shall never forget her response. "Rabbi," she said, "that's not the question. The important question is, 'What will I do with what I have left?'" That's strength at the broken places. That's resilience!

Second, Ruth quickly found ways of putting what she had learned to use to help others. Within months of her daughter's death, she and her husband were sitting in the living room of parents who had just lost a child, bringing comfort and insight to the newly bereaved. Compassion and wisdom Ruth never knew she had surfaced from the depths of her being. That's resilience!

Third, Ruth set her life into a larger context. She endeavored to see herself as God might see her. That's not easy to do, especially all by ourselves. My friend is bright and sensitive but, like all of us, she needed help. Being Jewish, Ruth turned to her faith community. She engaged in weekly study and prayer and embraced traditions that have enriched Jewish lives for generations. That's resilience!

I am not suggesting that there is a fixed formula for responding to tragic loss or to the challenges of growing old. Each of us must find the pathway that works best for us given the circumstances that we find ourselves in.

But whether you are Christian, Jewish, Hindu, Muslim, Buddhist or any tradition, you will find in your community pathways toward healing. Churches offer healing circles. Islamic centers provide study groups. Clergy can direct you to projects where you can help those in need and, at the same time, help yourself. Faith communities, family service agencies, and groups like IMAGINE extend a hand that helps to heal. Search out opportunities like these that enable you to put your life in a larger context. And as many studies indicate, you'll discover greater purpose in life and be a happier, more healthy person.

Viktor Frankl, who survived Nazi death camps, taught us that sometimes we cannot control what happens to us, but we can control how we respond (*Man's Search for Meaning,* Boston, Beacon Press, 1959). If we react to difficulty with courage and selflessness, if we try to do good for others, as my friend Ruth did, we achieve small victories over tough challenges.

As they often do, Psalms speak to us in times of distress:
"Weeping may endure for a night, but joy comes in the morning" (Ps. 30.5).

10. DISCOVERING PEACE

We are on this earth for a limited time. We can spend it tearing ourselves or others apart or we can use it to help others and enjoy the pleasures of life. One of my favorite Hebrew words is *shleimut.* It's a derivative of *shalom* (peace) and means wholeness, inner peace, completeness.

Here are a few pathways to *shleimut.*

Don't sweat the small stuff.
Most of it won't matter in ten minutes or in ten hours, so why let it take up a lot of your bandwidth.

Hug those closest to you.
Every day (as health factors permit). If you live alone and have limited contacts, hug someone over the phone, on FaceTime , or in your memory. If you are not a big hugger, then do it with words. If people are assisting you (such as a caregiver, repair person, sales clerk or health aide), tell them how much you appreciate their efforts.

Don't wait.
So you've always wanted to visit that town in the American Southwest, or that grand capital in Europe, or that nearby museum. Go for it as soon as you can. And don't wait to share those words of affection.

Forgive.
We all carry around emotional baggage, bitter memories and resentments that serve no purpose except to weigh us down. You may harbor resentment for a sibling, co-worker, supervisor, or one-time friend. You may have forgotten what that person did to anger you. But you've held on to that anger for years.

In the Torah, Joseph's brothers sold him into slavery. For 20 years he looked forward to getting even. Finally, the opportunity arrived and something strange happened. He tasted revenge and it turned bitter in his mouth. Joseph discovered that he did not enjoy it at all. When his brothers visited him in Egypt, he broke down and wept (Genesis 50.15-21).

In my career as rabbi and therapist, I have worked with dozens of individuals who have held on to grievances for a long time. Invariably, when they relinquish an old grievance and forgive another, they experience a physical sense of relief.

Holding on to grievances and nursing anger is comparable to carrying two heavy suitcases around for years. They weigh us down and keep us from traveling new pathways of life. When we discard them, we feel lighter, brighter, and eager to move forward. As F. Scott Fitzgerald observed: "Living well is the best revenge."

Give more than you receive.
 Consider this question: What was the nicest gift you received in the last year? Now ask yourself: What was the nicest thing that you did for someone else in the past year? Which gave you more pleasure? The gift you received or the one you gave?

Offer Gratitude.
I love the Hebrew expression: *hakarat haTov* – recognizing the good. The Talmud offers us a tool kit for gratitude. It instructs us to utter 100 blessings a day. It seems like so many. But if you start with *Motzee*, the Hebrew blessing for bread, or with the Christian Grace, and then thank God for the blue sky or seeing an old friend, you're on your "grateful way." Track it and see. The goal is not to jump suddenly to 100 blessings -- but to add *one* whenever you can.

The poet E.E. Cummings captured the art of the blessing:

> i thank You God for this most amazing
> day: for the leaping greenly spirits of trees
> and a blue true dream of sky; and for everything
> which is natural which is infinite which is yes
>
> (i who have died am alive again today,
> and this is the sun's birthday; this is the birth
> day of life and of love and wings: and of the gay great happening
> illimitably earth)
>
> (now the ears of my ears awake and
> now the eyes of my eyes are opened)

If you were building your ladder of blessings from the start, what would you give thanks for first? And after what would you express gratitude for second and third? As I write these lines, I am looking out over a beautiful lake where I behold magnificent sunsets. I think of Psalm 92:

> *Tov l'hodot la-Adonai,*
> *Ul'zamer l'shimcha elyon;*
> *L'hagid ba-boker chasdecha,*
> *Va-emuna-ticha ba-lailot.*

It is good to praise God
   To sing hymns to Your name, O most High.
To proclaim Your steadfast love at daybreak,
   Your faithfulness each night.

When we sing hymns to God, we make ourselves more grateful. Blessings are good for our health. Researchers at Virginia Commonwealth University School of Medicine discovered that high levels of thankfulness were associated with reduced risk for disorders like depression, phobias, and bulimia, as well as fewer antisocial personalities, and less alcohol and drug dependence. (Namica.org/blog/the-impact-of-gratitude-on-mental-health.) Some studies indicate that longer life expectancy is associated with thankfulness.

11. FINDING FAITH

For some, the mention of psalms or the word "faith" can be off-putting, conjuring up non-stop prayer ritual or rigid orthodoxy that strips away our autonomy. I urge you to think about faith in new and different ways. We find faith in many places:

In a Power beyond ourselves.
In a miraculously ordered system.
In a tradition of ethical living.
In community that supports, prays, and celebrates.
In songs of the spirit.
In moments of transcendence.
In acts of kindness.

Faith opens our eyes to a world larger than ourselves. It sustains us when we are down and emboldens us to be better than we are.

A member of our congregation in 1970 reminded me again and again that she was at least an agnostic, if not an atheist. Yet she insisted that she cherished our synagogue and Judaism.

Flash forward 48 years as she prepared to move to the Midwest to be with her daughter. At a Shabbat service in her honor, my agnostic/atheist friend ascended the pulpit and announced. "I am now a believer. I believe in this community and the social justice that it pursues. I believe in this synagogue and the support it has given me." She didn't once utter the word God, but rather talked about those qualities that we identify with God and the actions that we believe God expects of us.

Many people tell me, "Rabbi, I really don't believe in God." I then ask, "What kind of a God don't you believe in?" At which point, they describe a God who pulls strings from heaven controlling our lives;

or a God who brings illness upon the wicked; or a God who hears every prayer and responds, or does not respond, depending upon the level of our righteousness. "Guess what," I announce, "I don't believe in that kind of God either."

Faith comes in various shapes and sizes and it leads many a soul to goodness and justice. When s local Roman Catholic Church built a new campus at the intersection of two busy roads In Westfield, a prominent sign declared: "St. Helen's, A Catholic Community." No mention of Church. That sign, an Eye Opener to me, proclaimed to motorists, who were driving by, that community is often the pathway that brings us to faith. Community has many byways: small groups that teach by example, rituals that warm our soul, study that anchors belief, and music that elevates the spirit.

Legacies come in various shapes and sizes. One of mine is that our sons and daughter--Micah, Noah and Sarah--and their families found faith communities where they raised their children, served as synagogue trustees, and put Jewish values to work.

Community offers many platforms for *tikun olam,* repairing the world. One of those is to welcome the homeless. When our synagogue constructed in 2000 the Center for Jewish Learning which bears my name, a group of adult and youth members lobbied for a small shower room where our homeless guests could refresh themselves each morning instead of traveling to a "Y" eight miles away. That was an act of faith.

If you feed the hungry at your local soup kitchen or pack food for shipment to Africa because you believe that the Divine Spirit of the universe, whatever that may be, would not want any children to go hungry, that is an act of faith. If you work for the civil rights of Black and Brown people or the rights of members of the LGBTQ community because we are all created in God's image, that too is an act of faith.

12. CHOOSE YOUR BATTLES

Sneakers in a snowstorm

When our children were teens, Terry and I offered a workshop, "Raising Healthy Adolescents." That ambitious title revealed that we thought we knew more than we actually did. Despite our limited credentials and our audacious *chutzpah*, dozens attended our annual workshops until we grew too old to dare discuss that topic.

One memorable evening, a mother asked Terry what she should do about her "difficult 13-year-old" who insisted on wearing sneakers to school during a snowstorm. "He refuses to wear his galoshes (boots) and we argue about it all the time."

Terry's response came quickly: "No kid has ever died because he wore sneakers in the snow." That advice opened a few eyes. Ten years later, parents were still approaching Terry to thank her for her sage guidance. Terry's point was this: if you cut back on petty arguments, you open up the parental playing field to engage in more consequential topics.

Choose your battles carefully. That's good advice for marriage and the workplace. The husband who criticizes his spouse each time the scissors are misplaced loses credibility when the big issues arise that must be addressed. (Full disclosure: I've done that with the scissors.) The supervisor who focuses on a worker's shortcomings that are of little consequence will be poorly positioned to make constructive suggestions when something much more important pops up.

When Values Conflict: Canceling a United States Vice President

In the spring of 1972, the New Jersey Republican State Committee applied to Temple Emanu-El to rent our social hall for a large fundraiser. Our officers and I were instinctively hesitant, all the more when we learned that the guest speaker would be Vice-President Spiro Agnew. He and President Nixon were pursuing the Vietnam War that many of us opposed. However, as a religious institution, we felt that we must remain politically neutral. We asked ourselves: would we approve the rental request had it come from the Democratic State Committee? The answer was yes, so we agreed to the rental.

When our Senior Youth Group leaders learned that Agnew would speak in our building (though not under our auspices), they were outraged. A few days before the scheduled date, the group's president called early one morning to inform me that our teens planned to demonstrate outside their own temple on the night of the event and…would I join them?

I had to make a quick decision. (I hate making important decisions under time pressure.) My answer was "Yes."

At noon, as I drove home for lunch, I turned on Mutual News (then a major broadcast news outlet) and learned that "the rabbi of Temple Emanu-El in Westfield, New Jersey plans to join his teenagers in demonstrating against the Vice President when he arrives later this week at their temple."

I gulped down my lunch and raced back to my study, to be greeted by a call from the chair of the State Republican Committee. "Rabbi, how dare you demonstrate against us after your temple agreed to the rental. We are canceling our contract. We'll take our meeting to the Westfield Armory and…<u>you people should go back to where you came from.</u>"

I snapped back, "I'm gong to quote you on that."

"I'll deny it," he retorted and hung up.

The event took place, but at the Armory. The Veep flew into Newark and on to Westfield via secure military helicopter. As I reflect on this episode, I am struck by how many moral questions were involved.

1/ If a contract has been duly executed by the synagogue, does a temple group have the right to publicly oppose it?

2/ When political leaders engage in immoral acts, should they be opposed by every peaceful means possible? Where do we draw the line?

3/ When teenagers are motivated by the moral values we have taught them, should they be supported even if that conflicts with a decision of the trustees?

4/ Was Rabban Gamaliel correct: "Beware of the ruling power for they bring us near to them only for their own need; they do not stand by us when we are in distress"(*Ethics of the Fathers*, 2.3).

5/ What of Rabbi Hanina who seems to take a contrary view? "Pray for the ruling power, since but for fear of it, men would have swallowed up each other alive" (*Ethics of the Fathers*, 3.2).

6/ How would you react when someone, whether in public office or not, tells you "to go back to where you came from?" Is that clearly an anti-Semitic statement? Does that prejudice represent the thinking of an isolated individual, or does it reflect the attitude of something much larger that still exists 50 years later? If so, what is that "something larger?"

What other moral issues were involved? Could I have handled it better? How would you have dealt with this?

In retrospect, there may not have been a single right way. In the end, I found myself supporting our teens who ended up on the right side of history.

We later learned that it was the youth group president who had alerted Mutual News to the story. His family did not belong to our Temple. Subsequently, the bylaws of the youth group were modified to require that its officers be Temple members. Does that effect your thinking about how I should have responded?

A postscript. A few of our members were unhappy with our teens and with me. They asked our president to call a special meeting to allow concerned congregants to express their displeasure or even censure. A few dozen showed up. About six were critical. They had their moment. No one resigned and I went on to serve Temple Emanu-El an additional 30 years.

Sometimes We Must Speak Truth to Power

It was April 20, 1985 when President Ronald Reagan welcomed Elie Wiesel to the White House to accept the Congressional Gold Medal of Achievement. Wiesel, who would soon be awarded a Nobel Prize, had achieved worldwide acclaim. He could have sat back, basked in glory, and enjoyed an evening of undiluted praise.

Instead, as he rose to accept the award, he turned to the President who was scheduled to leave in two weeks for Germany to visit the German military cemetery at Bitburg where Nazi storm troopers were buried. In words we must not forget, Wiesel declared, "The issue here is not politics, but good and evil. And we must never confuse them. For I have seen the SS at work. And I have seen their victims. That place, Mr. President, is not your place. Your place is with the victims of the SS."

Remember the Biblical story in which the Hebrew prophet, Nathan, confronts King David who had an affair with Batsheva and arranged for the murder of her husband, Uriah. At God's command, Nathan tells the king the story of a rich man who slaughtered a poor man's only lamb. David is appropriately upset about this injustice, at which point Nathan announces, "You are the man" (2 Samuel 12.7). As Nathan called out King David, so Wiesel spoke truth to Reagan: your place is not with the perpetrators of evil, but with the victims.

Make no mistake about it. It is no easy matter to call out the King of Israel in his palace or the President of the United States in the Roosevelt Room of the White House. Wiesel did it respectfully, but firmly, confidant that he was reflecting the teachings of his faith and the painful history of his family and his people.

I frequently relive that moment in my mind. I treasure the courageous women and men who--with a sense of history--choose their battles wisely and speak truth to power, like civil rights activists Rosa Parks, Fannie Lou Hamer, John Lewis, and Dr. King, and Soviet dissident Natan Sharansky. More recently, Representatives Liz Cheney (R-WY), Jamie Raskin (D-MD), and Adam Schiff (D-CA).

Two weeks later, as Reagan toured the Bitburg military cemetery, Elie Wiesel was at our synagogue in Westfield fulfilling a previously arranged teaching commitment. (He taught annually at Temple Emanu-El for six years.) While a thousand people waited patiently in our Greifer Sacks Hall, Wiesel was 100 yards away, in my study, appearing on NBC's "Meet the Press." Via split screen television, he continued to speak truth to power while the President--on the other half of the screen--shamefully toured the grounds of Bitburg.

Think about your own experience. Have you ever been in a position where you felt the need to speak truth to someone in power? What were your feelings and what did you eventually do? Think of someone you know, personally or through reputation, whom you admire for speaking truth to power. What difference did that person make?

One of the best-known passages from Torah, emblazoned on tee shirts and empowering social activists, states *"Tzedek, tzedek, tirdof,* Justice, justice, shall you pursue"* (Deut. *16.20).* Since rabbinic tradition teaches that no word of Torah is superfluous, commentators ask why the word *tzedek* or justice is written twice. Rabbi Robert Marx of Chicago taught, "One *tzedek* calls me to explore how my Jewish values hold me accountable to pursuing justice, and one *tzedek* compels me to ensure my Jewish community is doing the same" ("The Second Tzedek," Jewish Council on Urban Affairs, Sept. 14, 2016).

Building on Rabbi Marx's interpretation, we can say that one *tzedek* expects us to speak truth to ourselves and one *tzedek* compels us to speak truth to power. We must start with ourselves, but we dare not end with ourselves.

13. GOVERNMENT OF THE PEOPLE

"We the People"

When Abraham Lincoln dedicated the Soldiers National Cemetery at Gettysburg, November 19, 1863, he memorably declared that ours is a government "of the people, by the people, for the people." Terry and I take each of our grandchildren to Washington for their tenth birthday. Together we stand before those words engraved on the wall of the Lincoln Memorial and discuss their meaning.

Decades before Gettysburg, the Framers of the Constitution commenced the Preamble with the words, "We the People." Every nation must determine who is sovereign. Upon that decision, all else rests. The Framers made it clear--reinforced by Lincoln--that it is not a president nor monarch, not an oligarch nor even a legislature that is supreme, but rather it is "We the People." Because "We the People" are foremost in our democratic republic, we are free to assemble, to march, to protest, to petition, and to speak truth to power.

In the summer of 1963, Dr. King summoned "We the People" to the March on Washington for Jobs and Freedom. King's call captured my attention. My spirit soared that early morning of August 28 as we welcomed congregants onto our buses. I exclaimed, "You care, you really, really care."

I have relived that day again and again over decades because I saw up close, eyeball to eyeball, what a difference 250,000 peaceful souls--Black and White, rich and poor--could make. One of the largest rallies for human rights in our nation's history, the March played an oversized role in the passage of the Civil Rights Act of 1964.

Dr. King's "I Have A Dream" speech that day circled the globe, inspiring millions and spawning countless initiatives. One of those initiatives was the Westfield/Plainfield "Dreamers" project described above.

Silence Is Not An Option

Preceding King on the dais at the Lincoln Memorial that warm August Wednesday was my neighbor in New Jersey, Rabbi Joachim Prinz. His stern warning was a clarion call to action:

> "When I was the rabbi of the Jewish community in Berlin, under the Hitler regime, I learned many things. The most important thing that I learned under those most tragic circumstances was that bigotry and hatred are not the most urgent problem. The most urgent, the most disgraceful, the most shameful and the most tragic problem is silence."

Each of us needs to consider the times when we were silent in face of injustice. When should we have spoken up, but did not? When could we have made a difference, but hesitated and backed off?

Most of us have had the unpleasant experience of hearing a friend, family member, or co-worker utter ethnic or racial slurs against Blacks, Hispanics, Asians, or Jews. How did we react? Were we proud of the way we did or did not respond? If you could relive that moment now, would your response be different?

When President Donald Trump rescinded regulations that protected our environment, when he praised white supremacists and anti-Semites in Charlottesville, when he assured us that the scourge of Covid19 would end in weeks, when he transformed the Attorney General into his own private lawyer, when he incited insurrection, where were we the people? Did we speak truth to power? Did we take action to express our outrage, to work for an enlightened political candidate, or to support an organization that fights for human rights?

Isabel Wilkerson describes July 6, 1940 when Hitler returned to Berlin for a conqueror's welcome after the Germans vanquished Paris in the battle of France. It seemed like every German was cheering Hitler. "They were human, insecure and susceptible to the propaganda that gave them an Identity to believe in, to feel chosen and important" (*Caste,* New York. Random House, 2020).

What would you have done had you been in their place? What would any of us have done? To what extent are Americans today susceptible to similar propaganda? How many of our fellow citizens are looking for "an identity to believe in, to feel chosen and important" no matter what darkness that search might take them to?

14. MAKING A DIFFERENCE

What Can One Person Do?

You may wonder what a single individual can do when the problems we confront are so overwhelming. Rabbi Tarfon in *Ethics of the Fathers* (2.16) anticipates our question: "It is not your duty to complete the task, but neither are you free to desist from it altogether."

Social remedies sometimes begin from the top down, but most originate from the bottom up. The impetus for civil rights legislation came from the Edmund Pettus Bridge in Selma, Alabama and the Ebenezer Baptist Church in Atlanta. Opposition to the Vietnam War came not from policy makers in Washington, but from student demonstrators on the campus of Kent State University in Ohio, and from mothers and sons protesting military conscription.

They were regular people singing John Lennon's "Give Peace a Chance," which hit the airwaves in 1966. The one hundred thousand people protesting the war at the Lincoln Memorial in October 1967 were regular people. So too were those flawed, but spiritually outraged souls protesting the war at the Democratic National Convention in Chicago 1968.

These regular people knew, like Rabbi Tarfon, that they could not finish the task. But this did not prevent them, imperfect though they were, from taking action. Without women or men carrying placards on the street and citizens waiting five hours to vote, without students on campus or outraged souls in the pews, peace and progress remain a dream. Without the 200,000 volunteers who mentor, chaperone, feed, and support the clients of Family Promise, many more homeless would be living on the streets and under the bridges of America's cities.

Can Religion Play a Pivotal Role in Changing America?

In my early years as a rabbi, I was convinced that, when people of faith collaborate, we could literally change the world. And I had evidence to prove that.

"Clergy and Laymen Concerned" was formed in 1965 for the purpose of ending U.S. military activity in Vietnam. That multi-racial faith-based network had an outsized impact on bringing the war to an end, although it took far too long to accomplish.

"Interfaith Coalition for the Homeless" (later Interfaith Hospitality Network and then Family Promise) was born in the boardroom of Christ Church in Summit, NJ, nurtured at Temple Emanu-El of Westfield, and powered by tens of thousands of persons of faith. The Civil Rights Act of 1964 and the Voting Rights Act of 1965 were drafted in the conference room of the Religious Action Center of Reform Judaism (RAC) in Washington, DC.

In the 1960s and 70s, seven out of ten Americans were affiliated with a religious group and some of those people of faith were changing the world. However, in 2021 Gallup poll reported that only 47% of Americans said that they belonged to a synagogue, church, or mosque. Does that mean that the faith community is now too weak to make a difference? Are people of faith no longer strong enough or unified enough to apply our moral values to the social, political, and economic problems of our times?

I do not buy that negative response. Here's a small example of what regular people of faith can do. In 2020, the NJ-RAC led the effort to enact "Ban the Box" legislation in New Jersey. The bill requires most New Jersey residential landlords to remove questions regarding a potential tenant's criminal history from initial applications for housing. This allows applicants the opportunity to tell the landlord their story of *t'shuva*--personal repair--instead of being rejected sight unseen. This is a fine example of people in the pews applying religious values to social problems. Thousands of similar success stories abound across our nation. Are you aware of some in your own religious community or one nearby? What are those stories and what difference have they made?

Alexis de Tocqueville was a keen observer of 19th century American life. From his extensive travels, he discovered that Americans practice democracy through local institutional leadership, town meetings, municipal government, and religious communities. He recognized that in a nation as vast as the United States, our circle of influence is minimal and it is difficult to make an impact. But, he taught, if you will draw a smaller circle and focus on that, within that circle you are powerful and you are free. Search for those local sweet spots where you can impact for good. Draw a circle around them and make a difference in that space.

Dr. King put it another way: "If you can't fly then run, if you can't run then walk, if you can't walk then crawl, but whatever you do...you have to keep moving forward."

Synagogues, churches, and mosques outnumber schools in America by 3:1. They are not all of one mind. And plenty of extremism is born and bred in right-wing Christian nationalism. But think of this: if just one quarter of Americans who affiliate with religious life were to join the battle for social justice, we could mobilize an army of tens of millions whom policy makers could not ignore. I urge you to be one of those who engages with the critical challenges of our time:

Global warming
Voter suppression
Racism
Gun Safety
Income inequity
Poverty

Health Care
Education
Anti-Semitism
Women's Reproductive Rights

Sometimes the challenge arrives unannounced.

15. PRINCIPLE KNOCKS AT THE DOOR

I had barely arrived in Westfield when conscientious objectors (COs) appeared at my door. They were mostly young men of draft age who had grown up in our synagogue and who now turned to their new rabbi for counsel and support. The Selective Service System, responsible for drafting young American men for military service, allows an exemption for persons who refuse to bear arms on moral or religious grounds.

My eyes were opened early one morning when a recent college graduate arrived without an appointment. He sought my help to explain to his parents why his car was parked outside our synagogue, loaded with personal possessions and fully fueled for a trip to Canada later that day!

About the same time another young man asked me to appear with him before the local draft board to support his petition for a CO exemption. One week later, I listened as draft board members probed: "If your family were threatened by an intruder, would you use a weapon to defend them? If a disturbed individual attacked you, would you fight back or let him injure or kill you?"

For a 19-year-old, these were tough questions, designed to determine whether his claim of conscientious objection was a convenient excuse to avoid the draft, or whether it flowed from deeply held religious faith. He navigated the labyrinth of questions well. I was there to explain to the Board that not all of my students were motivated by religious belief. Some were driven by powerful moral principles and those too, I argued, qualified as conscientious objection. Years later, some of those young men wrote from Canada, California, and New Jersey to express gratitude for the support they received.

What if you were called by your country to serve in the armed forces? Would your response be an immediate yes or would you ask yourself some questions and, if so, what might they be? Do you have friends or family who, if they were called to military service, might qualify as conscientious objectors? How do you feel in general about the CO exemption? Many CO's were absolute pacifists, but not all. Pacifism covers a wide spectrum. Those nuances are still relevant in our nation today.

Pete Seeger

Pete Seeger (1919-2014) was a man of principle. An acclaimed American folk singer and social activist, Seeger popularized protest music, placing his voice and his life on the line for military disarmament, civil rights, the environment, and opposition to the Vietnam War. His iconic songs, "Where Have All the Flowers Gone?" and "If I Had a Hammer," gave stirring voice to the Civil Rights movement and the anti-Vietnam War campaign.

Toward the end of my three-year stint as rabbi in Westbury, NY, I supported a local organization that invited Seeger to appear on behalf of the anti-Vietnam war movement which he inspired. The group signed a contract with the Board of Education in neighboring East Meadow to rent the W. Tresper Clark High School auditorium for $100 for the March 12, 1966 event. A week before the program, the Board received a complaint that Seeger was controversial and quickly moved to void the contract, based on the possibility of property damage (*Los Angeles Times*, Jan. 28 2014).

Although a lower court upheld the Board's action, the New York State Court of Appeals ruled in favor of the concert association. It declared that, while the Board had the right originally to deny the rental, once it had entered into contract, it would be an act of discrimination against Seeger's views to void the agreement. By then, the original date had come and gone. The Board argued that the case was therefore moot. New York State's highest court disagreed, maintaining that freedom of speech was too important to let the calendar interfere. The concert was held one year later. While 300 protested outside, 1100 fans packed the auditorium.

This was the first of several important legal actions that I was involved in that convinced me that the American judicial system is the bedrock of our democracy. A judiciary free of political interference or corrupt influence is essential to preserving the basic rights that underpin our democracy. The ancient rabbis taught, "Every judge who judges with complete fairness, even for a single hour, tradition gives that judge credit as though they had become a partner to the Holy One in the Creation" (Babylonian Talmud, *Shabbat* 10a). My faith in the judiciary has been validated again and again on the local scene and beyond.

Precisely because we Jews and all Americans have depended so much on an independent judiciary, so is our disappointment today so great. As I note below, the increasing politicization of the judiciary presents a grave threat to the future of our nation

The Christmas Pageant

Even before I settled into Westfield in 1966, Temple leaders informed me: "We have to do something about the Christmas pageant." "Art Masterpieces," as it was known, was a product of three departments of Westfield High School--art, music, and drama--and consisted of a series of tableaux of religious paintings accompanied by sacred music.

When the student choir sang the "Hallelujah Chorus" from Handel's *Messiah*, the audience stood without applause, as you would expect at a church service. Any student who wished to enroll in the popular chorus course was obligated to participate in the pageant.

C.A.R.E.S, Committee Against Religious Encroachment in Schools, was formed by local Christians and Jews. They brought a lawsuit in federal court against the Westfield Board of Education alleging violation of the separation of church and state. This action engendered anti-Semitic outbursts and threats of boycotts. Jewish merchants lost business and doctors lost patients. The *Westfield Leader* published references to "strangers in our town." Parents who supported the litigation felt the need to walk their children to school each day for fear of verbal assaults or worse.

Both sides appeared before Judge Frederick B. Lacey of the U.S. District Court in Newark who ultimately issued a consent decree ordering that the pageant would no longer be presented in its current form, nor would any Westfield schools present programs, "the purpose of which is the advancement of any religion or all religions." It was important to learn about all religions, but not to advocate for any nor to create a religious atmosphere as part of the fulfillment of curriculum. It was not a matter of numbers, declared Judge Lacey, but of law.

Once again, the courts protected the freedoms enshrined in the Constitution and communal peace returned to Westfield until....

The Parking Lot

Thirty years later we were back in court. This time the issue was the expansion of the Temple's parking lot.

As Temple Emanu-El grew to 1200 family units, it became clear that we needed to expand our parking area in order to remove cars from the streets and create a safer environment for Temple members, guests, and our neighbors. When the lot contiguous to the Temple became available, we recognized it as a once-in-a-lifetime opportunity and moved to acquire it, though at a steep cost.

When we informed neighbors of our plans and solicited their input, we were met with a combination of legitimate concerns (lighting, landscaping, traffic patterns), and vitriolic anti-Semitic rage. Many of us were dismayed. Was this the Christmas pageant *redux*? Not quite.

The Westfield Board of Adjustment denied the Temple application by 4-3. (Four votes were in favor, but the law required five.) But unlike the Christmas pageant 30 years earlier, the landscape had changed. Local clergy and neighbors defended the Temple.

After the denial, we once again sought judicial relief, maintaining our plan satisfied all requirements for the variance requested. We based our case on the Religious Land Use and Institutionalized Persons Act (RLUIPA) and our constitutional right to the free exercise of religion. In the spring of March 2005, Union County Assignment Judge Walter Barisonek approved a settlement that upheld our cause.

This time the vitriol subsided quickly, the rule of law prevailed, and peaceful relations rapidly returned. In the words of attorney Steve Barcan, a passionate advocate for the Temple, "Westfield was able to reject bigotry and emerge stronger than before."

The Torah and traditional Jewish commentaries are packed with high expectations for judges. Leviticus lays the foundation: "You shall not render an unfair decision. Do not favor the poor or show deference to the rich; judge your kinsman fairly" (19.15). A renowned 17th century Torah commentator is more specific. "Judges should not show favoritism, even to those who appointed them. Judges should judge all the people justly" (Rabbi Shlomo Ephraim ben Aaron Luntschitz on Deuteronomy 16.18). Although this dictum flows from Jewish sources, it clearly applies to every civil court in our land, including our nation's highest court.

Rabbi Jacob ben Asher (14th Century) taught that through judges who decide between people, the world endures, "because were it not for law, the more powerful would conquer" (Tur, *Choshen Mishpat* 1).

Much of secular law can be traced to Torah and rabbinic commentary. If we expect that justice will underpin American society, we must depend on the rule of law.

It is clear today that, on national and state levels, the rule of law is threatened. Basic human rights, including women's reproductive freedom and voting rights, are being eroded across the nation. Rampant political polarization threatens the integrity of our legislatures and our courts, against the will of "We the People."

Westfield 1966, rich in colonial history, was a leafy bastion of white mainline Protestantism, where minorities were tolerated, but marginalized. A glaring exception was the First Congregational Church that has partnered with Temple Emanu-El since the synagogue's inception in 1950. Today, Westfield is a remarkable work in progress, slowly becoming a healthy amalgam of diverse ethnic, racial, gender, and political identities. Town leadership today is humane and visionary. Clergy and lay leaders are enlightened and progressive.

When anti-Semitic boycotts erupted in 1972, in response to the Christmas pageant imbroglio, I stood in the second floor meeting room of a church where I appealed to Westfield's senior clergy to stand united against the outpouring of hate with, at least, a strong statement against anti-Semitism. The response was...deafening silence! I stared out the window overlooking the Lord & Taylor parking lot and turned to my good friend, Fr. Sal Tagliareni, then a priest at Holy Trinity Church. "Sal," I said, "if the Nazis were rounding up Jews in that parking lot right now, I believe you would be among the few to defend us."

69

That is not true today. Not even close. Most of the women and men who today lead the religious institutions of Westfield are cut from a different cloth. They abhor racism; they disdain anti-Semitism; they detest misogyny; they will not tolerate homophobia; they lift up the poor; they advocate for the prisoner; they feed the hungry and support the orphan. Their eyes have been opened by the teachings and life work of giants of the religious spirit.

16. THE ARC BENDS TOWARD JUSTICE

Anti-Semitism. It Never Seems to End

One of those giants, Dr. Martin Luther King, Jr., taught that "the arc of the moral universe is long, but it bends toward justice." (Rev. Theodore Parker first coined the phrase in 1853.) We have seen the arc bending toward justice in our synagogue and throughout the interfaith community where clergy leadership, not perfect and often slow to respond, today reflects the teachings of giants like Abraham Joshua Heschel, Paul Tillich. Dietrich Bonhoffer, and Reinhold Niebhur.

Yet, with all of this progress, swastikas and racial slurs have been etched on walls and sidewalks of some Westfield schools and streets. Students of color, Jews, and Asians report harassment. These deplorable actions do not reflect the Westfield that I have seen emerge in the last two decades where citizens reject hate and come together in large numbers to support diversity.

On the national scene and beyond, political extremists, white supremacists, and anti-Semites are hard at work. Attacks on Jews and Jewish institutions in America are at a record high. The worst massacre of Jews in American history occurred in 2018 at Tree of Life synagogue in Pittsburgh. The following year one person was killed and three injured, including the rabbi, in an attack on the Chabad of Poway Synagogue in California. An Austin temple was firebombed in 2021, while a few months later my Reform colleague, Rabbi Charlie Cytron-Walker, and three others were held hostage on Shabbat morning in Colleyville, Texas. Days later, the scholar of the Holocaust, Deborah Lipstadt, wrote in *The New York Times* that some rabbis' children don't want them to be congregational rabbis anymore. "It's too dangerous."

The hostage-taker proclaimed a canard that sadly has a long shelf life, that "Jews control the world." That dangerous anti-Semitic trope was used by Hitler's Nazi regime post World War One to explain all of Germany's woes.. That heinous falsehood was at the core of a widely circulated, vicious anti-Semitic tract, *The Protocols of the Elders of Zion*, and central to the national radio broadcasts in the 1930s of Fr. Charles Coughlin whose anti-Jewish diatribes were heard by 30 million listeners.

Paul Krugman captured the strategy of anti-Semites and white supremacists: "When the people are suffering, you don't try to solve their problems, instead, you distract them by giving them someone to hate" (*New York Times*, April 19, 2022).

Jewish institutions globally must be laser focused on security. We must balance two virtues that are now in conflict: be an open, welcoming *bet knesset*, a holy place of gathering, and, at the same time, be a safe and secure center for Jewish life. We must call out the big anti-Semitic lie every time it appears and we must insist that our inter-faith colleagues and public officials do the same.

After the Colleyville attack, our local Christian clergy showed up at Shabbat services to demonstrate their solidarity with their Jewish sisters and brothers. At the 2022 Martin Luther King, Jr. memorial service, Westfield's mayor, Shelley Brindle, used the occasion to call out both racism and anti-Semitism. They are interconnected and Dr. King knew it.

The Westfield Hall of Fame in 2019 was memorable, not because a rabbi was one of the inductees, but because a Black man, Paul Robeson (1898-1976), was posthumously honored. It took much too long for Westfield to recognize its native son, a renowned singer, football All-American at Rutgers, and civil rights activist who was blacklisted during the McCarthy era. A little late, to be sure, but as King taught us, "the arc of justice...is long."

It took 233 years until a Black woman would take her seat as an associate justice on the Court. At last, on the White House lawn, the day after the U.S. Senate confirmed her appointment in April 2022, Ketanji Brown Jackson offered these words of Dr. Maya Angelou: "I am the dream and the hope of the slave." Very late, but "the arc...is long."

Jackson's appointment notwithstanding, public confidence in the United States Supreme Court has dramatically eroded, and for good reason. When the Court overturned Roe v. Wade, it said to the vast majority of the American people, we don't care what you think, what you feel, or what you need. We don't give a damn about the American people and precedents that have served our democracy and our citizens well for half a century and beyond. No wonder our highest courts feel disconnected from the will of the people.

Clearly, the arc does not inevitably move in one direction. Its mythically optimistic tone can easily lull us into believing that there is some Divine assurance that goodness and justice will prevail. I used to believe that, but no longer. That will only happen if we all do our part—each and every one of us—to bend the arc forward.

Since the Court turned the clock back on women's reproductive rights, I have seen a groundswell of response from clergy, parents, elected officials, women of all ages, and so many more. They are intent on bending the arc. They take action with no guarantees of success. But they cannot live with themselves without making the fullest effort to reverse this travesty of justice.

Try asking yourself each morning: what am I gong to do today to bend the arc toward kindness and justice?

Abraham Joshua Heschel

Temple Emanu-El's weekly seminar in Bible and Jewish Thought is probably one of the longest running, uninterrupted classes of its kind in America, 67 years and counting. For much of the time that I taught the class, the Jewish thinker who repeatedly opened the eyes of our learners was Rabbi Heschel.

Heschel's insights are uniquely accessible. A scion of several Hasidic dynasties, Heschel uses imagery and poetry to bring us closer to the Divine. The titles of his foundational books reveal the direction of his thought: *Man's Quest for God, God in Search of Man, Man Is Not Alone* and *Sabbath.* (Yes, Heschel too was trapped in non-inclusive gender language.)

One pathway to God is to discover the Divine spark in every human being. That led Heschel to become a social activist and a spiritual partner of Dr. King. In 1965, Heschel joined King in the historic march from Selma to Montgomery, Alabama. On his return, someone asked the rabbi if he found time to pray in Selma. Heschel's memorable reply: "I prayed with my feet."

That response opened many eyes. It taught people of every faith that, in addition to traditional prayer, we pray building houses with Habitat for Humanity, marching with Black Lives Matter, advocating for sensible gun laws, and comforting the bereaved. When we recite a blessing *and* become a blessing, we enter into relationship with God.

Few Are Guilty. All Are Responsible

Heschel famously taught: "Few are guilty. All are responsible."

Karen Olson did not feel guilty, but she did feel responsible. Her job with a New Jersey pharmaceutical company brought her to New York City once or twice a week. As she passed through the Port

Authority Bus Terminal in 1985, she noticed the growing number of homeless. Unlike other travelers, Karen stopped to talk with them and learned that they were hungry most of the time.

Karen was not guilty. But she felt responsible to do something. She and her children made sandwiches in their Summit, New Jersey home, traveling to the Bus Terminal on weekends to distribute them. Karen quickly recognized that "sandwich trips" to the terminal were not enough. As a woman of faith and a committed Christian, she envisioned that the religious community of Union County could be mobilized to assist the homeless.

With that vision, Karen opened the eyes of the compassionate in synagogues, churches, and mosques, social service agencies and corporations.

What began as a collaboration of 11 local congregations has grown into Family Promise, a national network with more than 200+ Affiliates that has served more than one million persons, the majority children.

In the spirit of Heschel, Karen embodied responsibility. When a few of us--rabbis, ministers, priests--sat with Karen, we were energized by her passion, compelled by her moral imperative, impressed by her strategic savvy, and amazed by her spirituality.

Whoever Saves One Life...

The Talmud teaches, "Whoever saves one life it is as if that person saved the whole world" (Talmud, *Sanhedrin* 37a).

How is that possible? How can a single person save the entire world? Here's one way that I saw it work: Karen's humanity and her strategy for saving lives were offered for a dozen of us to behold.

We in turn brought that vision to dozens more. They proceeded to mobilize a task force to repair a big piece of our world.

The churches, synagogues, and mosques of our nation--when mobilized and focused--can change the world. We speak with pride about our Judeo-Christian heritage and we trot it out to celebrate at interfaith services, the birthday of Dr. King, and Thanksgiving. But what happens the rest of the year? I have learned more about the faith of my Christian sisters and brothers by working side-by-side fighting homelessness and opposing the Vietnam War than by decades of Thanksgiving observances.

Rev. Keary Kincannon taught that "relationships with poor people are converting. My experience is that middle-class churches that open their hearts to the poor benefit at a deep spiritual level as much as the poor benefit from the bricks and mortar" (*Building on Faith: Models of Church Sponsored Affordable Housing Programs in the Washington, DC Area* (Washington DC, the Churches Conference on Shelter and Housing, 1989, ii).

I spent one night as a chaperone at our Temple's homeless shelter, assisting our guests and sleeping on a cot. I awoke at sunrise, checked in with our breakfast crew, and headed home. I shall never forget the feeling as I traveled down our street and our home came into view. I was overwhelmed by the sense of being blessed. I was filled with gratitude for my wife and children, for the comfortable bed on which to rest my head, for nutritious meals, and for the stability of my existence. I felt spiritually transformed by that night in our shelter and emboldened to do more.

I thought of the passage from our prayer book. "It is one thing to be blessed. It is another to know that we are blessed." That was a night of spiritual amazement. As Heschel taught, "Radical Astonishment opens our eyes to the Divine."

17. THE POWER OF RELIGIOUS COMMUNITY

Eyes Open! Something Amazing Is Happening.

When I arrived in Westfield in 1966, the construction of our large sanctuary and social hall was nearing completion. But the artistic ornamentation for the façade, which faced heavily trafficked East Broad Street, was still under discussion. The Building Committee turned to me for suggestions and together we agreed upon a verse from the Hebrew prophet, Micah, Chapter 6, verse 8.

Over the years, as I walked by the façade, I would often pause to contemplate the deeper meaning of the verse:

"Do Justly.
Love Mercy.
Walk Humbly With God.

But with the passage of time, as frequently happens, I started to take the verse for granted. As I neared retirement, something unusual occurred: letters and comments about the Micah passage began arriving.

From a Temple leader: "I have always appreciated the words affixed to the front of our building. If we keep that message front and center--as individuals and as a synagogue--we're going to be fine."

From a non-Jewish neighbor of the synagogue: "I run by the front of the Temple each day and never fail to take in the words of Micah."

From a former Westfield resident who led civic organizations: "When I lived in Westfield, I regularly passed Temple Emanu-El. The verse from Micah grounded me and helped to get me on track. It told me where to focus."

From a Protestant minister: "Your verse from Micah sums it all up. It's what binds us together in a religious community. I need to thank you for placing it where you did for all to see."

I thought of the Biblical Jacob. Traveling from Haran to Beersheba, he lay down to sleep and dreamt of a ladder with angels ascending and descending. On waking, he declared, "How awesome is this place, and I did not know it" (Genesis, Ch. 28). How awesome is the verse from Micah and I had begun to take it for granted.

Sometimes amazing things are happening before our eyes and we do not know it. Who could imagine that a verse on our façade would become a moral compass not only for our congregants, but for commuters, runners, ministers, board members, and others whose names are unknown to me. You never know what an impact a few words or a kind deed may have. A passer-by is inspired to address food scarcity. Other communities replicate her vision. A national program emerges and millions in need enjoy nourishing meals. A few words, a good deed, can save the world.

Moral Compass Everywhere

How does a synagogue, church, or mosque become a moral compass? How does a friend, relative, or public figure become a moral mentor?

Keep your eyes open for religious communities that address the burning moral issues of the day. Pay attention to the church or synagogue board of trustees or enlightened member, the pastor, imam, or rabbi who stand up for those who have no one to speak for them. Here are two examples of moral leadership from our synagogue trustees. I select them only because I know our local scene best. There are thousands of inspiring examples, many in your neighborhood. Search them out. They deserve to be supported celebrated, and replicated.

When our courageous Jewish brothers and sisters in the Soviet Union were awakening to the possibility of freedom, it became important to send a clear, unmistakable message that Temple Emanu-El stood with them shoulder to shoulder. Our social justice activists organized a first-ever march down Westfield's main thoroughfare to mobilize the community. Hundreds of adults and children of all faiths responded.

Keep in mind that the Temple was only 20 years old and the Jewish community had confronted several polarizing struggles with anti-Semitism. Yet our Temple leadership did not hesitate for a moment to take to the streets, peacefully and lawfully, to support a cause that had a moral claim upon us.

One march for justice yields another and then another. They add up. They impact a community. They influence policy makers. They can save a segment of the world.

A second example of instinctive moral leadership occurred when we proposed that the Temple host homeless women and families. Not all congregations that we asked agreed to participate. The plan called for each house of worship to host in their building overnight up to 15 adults and children six weeks a year, including meals, tutoring, and recreation. Some demurred citing insufficient space or sanitation and security concerns. Leaders with a moral compass found a way to Yes, determined to apply their values to address an urgent human need.

18. MENTORS

It helps to have mentors. We all need a few wise, righteous souls to show us the way.

As a philosophy major studying the writings of Martin Buber, I was attracted to Buber's concept of the "I and Thou." He contrasts "I and Thou" with "I-It." The latter occurs in most situations where we relate to something or someone as a thing or an "It." The "It" is an instrument to get something done. We climb into our car, start the engine, and drive. Nothing special. We simply utilize the automobile—the "It"--to get from point A to point B. Or we enter a store and interact with the clerk by handing her cash or a credit card. Again, nothing special occurs other than a transaction.

"I and Thou" is different. When we relate to something or someone as a "Thou," we pause with intentionality, we enter into relationship, and we connect with a person's humanity with our entire being. We are in the moment. Buber teaches that the fullest meaning of life is in relationship.

We can also relate to a tree, a flower, or an animal as a "Thou." My wife and I do so every autumn when brilliant leaves light up the Northeast. The "I and Thou" relationship can last a fleeting second or much longer. In our encounter with a "Thou," Buber suggests, we can experience the Divine., which is the ultimate "Thou."

During my freshman year in college, I learned that Buber would be speaking at the Yale Law School. I hustled over late one weekday afternoon to find almost every seat occupied in the auditorium. I sat through the lecture, frustrated that I could comprehend only a fraction of Buber's talk, but awestruck to be in the presence of greatness.

I remained for the question period that turned out to be the capstone of my week. A petite, grey-haired woman in the fifth row was the first to be recognized. After asking her question haltingly in a deep German accent, she humbly concluded, "Doctor...Buber, do...you...understand...me?" The world famous philosopher locked his eyes onto hers in a visual embrace than seemed to affirm every ounce of her humanity. He paused, smiled slightly, and responded, "Yes, madam, I do."

In that amazing moment, it seemed that Buber had entered into an "I and Thou" relationship with a woman whom he had never met. In doing so, he affirmed her soul and her humanity in such an intimate and yet transcendent way that it felt as if God dwelt between them. It was then that I knew--not through words but through relationship--that Buber would be a moral mentor, a compass that could keep me on track at least some of the time, offering direction for my life's work.

Years later, as I taught thousands of confirmation class students, I related that story, seeking to engage my tenth graders--whose hormones were raging--in the art of the "I and Thou" dialogue. One of those students, Paul Jennis, captured Buber's riveting eyes in a portrait he sketched for his Confirmation project. While Paul has gone on to a distinguished career as artist and illustrator, his portrait of Buber hangs to this day in our breakfast alcove reminding me each morning to treat those dearest to me--and strangers as well--not as an "It," but as a "Thou." You will find Paul's rendition of Buber on the front cover of this book.

A moral mentor can be a parent, like my father who insisted that I return that ring from the hood of the Buick. Or my mother, whose resilience in old age, opened my eyes to the wonder of human adaptability.

Your mentor can be a colleague, such as the senior rabbi in my first pulpit at Temple Israel, Boston: Roland B. Gittelsohn, whose moral compass never wavered. Again and again, Roland challenged his congregants (and his junior colleague) to oppose nuclear escalation and racial discrimination. His passion for justice upset many and sometimes obscured his compassion, but he never blinked when confronting a critical moral choice. (A worthwhile read is Roland's 1945 dedicatory sermon at the U.S. Marine Corps Cemetery on the island of Iwo Jima following one of the bloodiest battles of World War II.)

Sometimes our mentor appears in literary form. One evening in 1964, my wife, Terry, looked up from a volume that had engaged her for many days and announced: "I think this book is about me!"

It was also about me. Betty Friedan's *The Feminine Mystique* is a significant marker on the liberation journey of the American woman, an odyssey that subsequently impacted men as well and specifically male rabbis like me.

Our mentors also appear as mesmerizing teachers. Professor Vince Scully, renowned historian of architecture and art, imbued me with an appreciation of great artistic works that has lasted a lifetime. For Scully, the purpose of architecture was not simply about the making of buildings, but about the making of civilized communities. Richard B. Sewall's literature course on tragedy opened my eyes to writers from Fyodor Dostoevsky to Arthur Miller who captured the pathos of life.

What books have you read that still mentor you? Who are the teachers who, years later, continue to instruct you? Which of your relatives impact you right now? And what difference have your mentors made in your life? How have they helped you to contribute your little bit to making our world a better place?

The Scottish poet Thomas Campbell wrote in his poem *Hallowed Ground*, "To live in the hearts we leave behind is not to die." Relatives, mentors, teachers, they all continue to live within our minds, hearts, and souls.

19. ASKING FOR MONEY

When I was a newly minted rabbi, on my list of the 20 activities frequently expected of me, the least favorable, #20, was asking for money. I had many reasons: I did not enjoy asking others to part with their hard earned cash. As a "spiritual" leader, it somehow seemed beneath me, or at least not compatible with my vision of the *rav* (rabbi).

I felt the angst of conflicting roles. Let's say a congregant came to me this week for pastoral counseling. How would I feel next month asking her for money? It could seem shabby, as if I were expecting a *quid pro quo*. What if I felt compelled to take a strong liberal stance on an issue of the day and was about to reach out to a conservative member for a large gift?

That angst subsided in the early 1980s when Temple leadership envisioned a building expansion. Our president, a wise mentor, encouraged me to ask a member, Ed Sacks for a large gift, assuring me that she would be right beside me when I made the "ask." In my study, Ed inquired how much we were seeking. I took a deep breath and blurted out a large number. He didn't blink an eye. "Rabbi," he said, "you have the hard job. You have to deal with a thousand members. All I have to do is write a check." To this day, Greifer Sacks Hall at Temple Emanu-El marks his family's legacy.

On that occasion and subsequently, mentors taught me enough about fund raising that I felt comfortable to pass those lessons on to my rabbinic students at HUC. Here are a few of them.

1/ Most people have a generous side to them. Many are simply never approached. By asking them to support a worthy cause, we honor them. No matter what words we choose, we send this message: I know that you care; I believe that you share many values and goals that I do. Let's do something transformational together. In this way, the rabbi can be a *shadchan* (matchmaker) for greatness. A philanthropist who responded positively to me once said, "I was waiting for you to ask!"

2/ When we ask, we give donors a chance to dream; we offer them an opportunity to leave an enduring legacy, to make a difference. By his gift, Ed honored his family, who were founding members, and enriched the Jewish community they gave birth to. The Book of Proverbs teaches *"Tz'dakah tatzil m'mavet,* Doing justly (read: giving to a worthy cause) saves us from death" (10.2). What is a legacy? It is a gift of the human spirit that we received from those before us and that we pass on to those who come after us. Our *tz'dakah* lives on after we are gone.

3/ Bring a partner. A partner softens the moment, gives you courage, and offers the donor another pathway if needed.

4/ If you're meeting with individuals who have significant resources, do not insult them by under asking. That doesn't serve their interests or yours. It is often easier to obtain a $1million gift than $10,000.

5/ And what about the caution that rabbis should stick to spiritual concerns? Rabbi Israel Salanter (1810-83), the founder of the *Musar* movement, taught that someone else's material concerns are my spiritual responsibility. That is, if someone needs food or shelter, it is my spiritual imperative to help. Similarly, when they require support for their children's Jewish education, their synagogue membership, or tuition to a Jewish summer camp, that need becomes my spiritual concern. Another way of putting it: Many people worry about their own stomachs and other people's souls. What they should worry about is other people's stomachs and their own souls.

Moses asked every Israelite "whose heart moves him" to give generously. He gathered the entire community to tell them that God expects donations of precious metals, fine yarns, valued skins, and gems to adorn the *Mishkan* or Tabernacle (Exodus, 35:4-9). Moses was the first fundraiser in Jewish history.

Rabbi Eleazar ben Azariah taught in *Ethics of the Fathers,* "If there is no dough, there is no study of Torah" (3.21). Read "dough" as a double *entendre*, money or the stuff for making bread. This teaches us not only that we need a full stomach to study Torah, but that we need to support the place where we learn and grow as Jews, namely, the synagogue. By the same token, this means support of church, mosque or another place of worship.

We Jews are blessed with multiple ways to serve God and the Jewish future: prayer, study, tradition, and acts of kindness. Through financial support of worthy causes, we also serve God.

We are currently living through a period of the largest transfer of personal wealth from one generation to another in human history. Baby boomers and their parents will transfer as much as $68 trillion in a period of 25 years. This means that some of our neighbors, friends, and fellow congregants are--or soon will be--searching for worthy causes. It is a privilege for a rabbi to engage with individuals who have discretionary resources and to offer suggestions for *tikun olam,* for improving the world.

20. MASCULINE DEPRIVATION.
LEARNING FROM WOMEN

Upon ordination in 1960, I was catapulted into an American liberal Judaism whose expectations of its rabbis had remained relatively static for generations. The sermon was central, decorum was obligatory, leadership was top-down, and success was measured by the size of one's congregation.

During one of my most formative periods, I spent eight years of study at two institutions: Yale and Hebrew Union College, where my classmates and professors all looked like me. Both were bastions of gender segregation and masculine superiority. (That all started to change 50 years ago.) Only recently have I come to appreciate how deprived I was by that draconian limitation.

In Biblical Hebrew, there are two words that describe fundamentally different aspects of the Divine. One is *Adonai* that refers to the softer, more compassionate aspect of God; the other, *Elohim*, is associated with God's firm, sometimes-stern justice. These can be described respectively as the immanent and transcendent aspects of the Divine.

My studies of Martin Buber nudged me toward the immanent and the more personal. But the available vocabulary for such a relationship was scarce. (In the patriarchal world, the feminine for Divine Presence, *Sh'chinah*, was rarely used.) Models of spiritual seekers were mostly hidden from view.

My dear friend, Rex Perlmeter, ordained in 1985, remembers reading an article by our colleague, Margaret Mors Wenig, in which she described conversing with God over tea at a kitchen table. Rex recalls: "I was astounded by the thought of such a way of experiencing the Divine, and I wanted it--not instead of my previous experience, but in addition to it. Theologically, I connected deeply with God, the Father and King. My teaching tended to the intellectual and my positioning to the authoritarian."

For Rex, these ways of being and thinking were not necessarily a result of the overt examples of his mentors, but were more reflective of the lens through which he interpreted their teaching.

According to Rex, "one of my mentors counseled me that I would only become the rabbi I ultimately had the potential to become if I could learn to bring a gentleness which was absent from my way of 'rabbi-ing.' The problem was that I didn't know where to look for mentors on how to do that. Most of my teachers embodied it fully and gracefully. My own perception of maleness, however, made it very difficult for me to emulate their bearing. I needed a different kind of role model. I needed women who were great rabbis to teach me how to become a man who could aspire to be a better rabbi" (excerpts from my chapter, "The Impact of Women Rabbis on Male Rabbis," in *The Sacred Calling: Four Decades of Women in the Rabbinate*, New York, CCAR Press, 2016).

As we gather our mentors, we must sometimes follow a trail. In my case, I traveled from my wife's insights to Betty Friedan to women rabbis who, by word and deed, have demonstrated that unless we live what we preach, we are bound to feel less than authentic. They taught us that the "Jewish family" begins with our own families which deserve the best that we can give them, not what is left over after we have visited every hospital in the region and polished a sermon for the 18th time.

Traditionally, men have placed less emphasis on establishing a healthy balance between personal life and work because, if they fell short on the family side, there was usually a spouse to carry that load. As women increasingly entered the workforce, men could enjoy that "privilege" less and less. Out of necessity, women and men now must achieve equilibrium and a new sense of what gender means.

Twenty-five years ago, a young female rabbi delivered a sermon in which she told a story from her own life experience. After the service, her senior rabbi, who was a man, asked, "How did it feel sharing that personal story with the congregation?" Until that time, he had felt forbidden to reveal anything personal about himself from the pulpit. Henceforth, he started to use his own life experience as a teaching tool.

With the help of this young colleague and many other women rabbis, the traditional and often self-imposed distance between rabbi and congregant has narrowed. Our female colleagues demonstrate that, by sharing our human side as well as our intellectual capacity, by engaging in deep and open relationships,, we can more effectively nurture and guide our community. (Martin Buber would have approved.)

Because of what we rabbis have learned from female colleagues, we have become better listeners, better nurturers, and better role models. When we are willing to share our personal side and to reveal our vulnerabilities, we become more approachable and more effective.

As a result of working closely with female colleagues, we have become more collaborative, more empathetic, less top down, and better listeners. I am tempted, for a moment, to suggest what my female colleagues might be learning from us men, but I shall quickly move on. It's not my place even to suggest. What I do recognize is that Reform Judaism in general, and Hebrew Union College in particular, transformed --even revolutionized—the role of gender in Judaism as we know it.

Great Women, Biblical and Beyond

Rabbi Priesand was ordained at the Cincinnati campus of HUC in 1972. As I write these words, the 50th anniversary of the ordination of our first female rabbi in North America is upon us. Sally is the second woman rabbi in Jewish history. The first was Regina Jonas who was ordained in Germany in 1935 and murdered by the Nazis at Auschwitz in 1944.

Shortly after my retirement, Sally called to ask if I would fill in for her during a three-month medical leave. During that brief time at nearby Monmouth Reform Temple, I learned close up that Sally had been an exceptional teacher, pastor, and leader for her synagogue and the wider community.

Kol hakavod (well done) to Rabbi Priesand and to Rabbi Nelson Glueck, President of HUC, who supported the admission and ordination of Sally Priesand. Sally should rank high in any list of female teachers and heroes of Judaism. Who would be on your list of women who have made a difference to you personally, or to your religion, whether it is Christianity, Judaism, Islam, or another? Take a moment to list their names.

My list includes:
The Matriarchs, Sarah, Rebecca, Rachel and Leah
Miriam
The Hebrew midwives, Shifra and Puah, who took care of the baby Moses.
Deborah
Ruth
Queen Esther
Bruriah, a scholar in Talmudic times.
Emma Goldman, social activist
Rabbi Regina Jonas

Hannah Szenes, poet and heroic anti-Nazi fighter.
Rabbi Sally Priesand

Mordecai Kaplan

During my freshman year at Yale, I started having second (and third) thoughts about becoming a rabbi. Challenged by my studies in philosophy, my adolescent faith in God began to wane. An all-powerful Creator who is a God of goodness should have been able to create a better world than the one where 70 million died in World War II, including six million Jews in the Holocaust.

For counsel, I turned to Stanley Rabinowitz, rabbi of New Haven's Congregation B'nai Jacob, where I was teaching tenth grade. Stanley recommended that I devote a chunk of the coming summer to books by Rabbi Mordecai Kaplan, the founder of the Jewish Reconstructionist movement and professor at the Jewish Theological Seminary.

Kaplan understood God not as a supernatural power, but as the force making for personal fulfillment and societal redemption. For Kaplan, the purpose of prayer was not to change God, but to change us. He described Judaism as an evolving religious civilization replete with language, culture, arts, literature, music, organizations, and a homeland. He believed that Jews are not "God's Chosen People," but rather a "God-Choosing People." By that he meant that Jews should make a conscious decision to pursue the ethical goals that, according to our tradition, the Divine has set for of us. Mordecai Kaplan was right about almost everything.

The First Bat Mitzvah

Kaplan argued for the equality of women in Judaism and on March 18, 1922, he officiated at the bat mitzvah of his daughter, Judith, at his Reconstructionist synagogue in New York City. It was probably the first time that a Jewish girl in America was called up to read from the Torah scroll. Later in life, Kaplan explained that he had four reasons for initiating the ceremony of bat mitzvah, namely, four daughters, Judith, Hadassah, Naomi and Selma.

Kaplan's Judaism felt more comfortable to me than the rarified theology that had been the underpinning of my rabbinical aspirations. Being a passionate Zionist, I also resonated with the centrality of Zion in Kaplan's Judaism.

Rabbi Rabinowitz could not have imagined what a gift he gave me. Nor could Mordecai Kaplan anticipate that he would rescue generations of rabbis and rabbinic students from their theological dilemmas, redirecting many of us from the pursuit of law, medicine, or an MBA.

From rabbinic student to active retired rabbi, I shall be forever grateful. You never know when a kind word, a smile, an arm on the shoulder, a book in your hand, a conversation over coffee can rescue a soul. I am grateful because, in the words of the historian Salo W. Baron, "by studying, applying and living Torah, the rabbi remains the chief protagonist in the drama of Jewish communal survival." It's a privilege that I might have missed.

21. GROWING INTO OUR DREAMS

Terry and I are lifelong Zionists. Our teenage Judaism was shaped, in large part, by Young Judaea, hers in Jacksonville, FL and mine in Atlanta. We were nourished on Hebrew songs, Israeli folk dance, debates, regional conventions, and a strong Jewish community, all of which Kaplan celebrated. I joined Young Judaea's first Summer-in-Israel program at age 15. Israel was three years old, conditions were harsh, and my mother was not happy.

We were based at Meir Shfeyah Youth Village in northern Israel where buzzing flies outnumbered Zionists by ten thousand to one. The joke in those years of primitive agriculture in Israel was about soup. The first time you're served soup with a fly in it, you throw out the soup and the fly. The second time, you toss the fly and eat the soup. On third go around, you eat the soup <u>and</u> the fly!

I gained a teenager's insight into the nascent state and the Jewish people when dysentery landed me in Shfeyah's infirmary. My roommate was a young boy newly arrived from Iraq. We had no common language, but that didn't keep us from bonding, joking, and lifting each other's spirits. I learned the meaning of "*Kol Yisrael arevim zeh bazeh*, all Jews are responsible one for the other."

That was my first encounter with a Jew of color and a hint of what the future held. Sixty-five years later, I was met with incredulity when I explained to a seminar I was leading that 12 to 15 percent of the Jews of America were persons who did not look like us. By then, HUC was ordaining Jews of color and inter-racial marriages were no longer unusual among American Jews. In a 2021 Pew study, 13% of American Jews reported that they lived in multi-person households where at least one individual was of a different race or ethnicity than the respondent.

Lacey Schwartz Delgado, whose mother withheld from her the fact that her biological father was Black, feels that society was "telling us that being Black and Jewish was…almost diametrically opposed" (*New York Jewish Week*, May 6, 2022).

We are still learning the meaning of Jewish pluralism. For decades, it referred to denominational branches, like Reform, Conservative, and Orthodox. Now, pluralism is an exciting—and demanding-- work in progress, We Jews, who were redeemed from Egyptian slavery, must now appreciate and engage with Jews of every color, gender identity, ethnic origin, physical ability, and theological persuasion or lack thereof.

Amos, one of the most important Hebrew prophets, teaches that God is color-blind: "To Me, O Israelites, you are just like the Ethiopians" (9.7), Ethiopians of course are people of color.

In 1958, I returned to Israel with Terry, as part of my rabbinic studies. At Hebrew University, we attended a Hebrew *ulpan,* an intensive, immersive program to master the language. Two months into the *ulpan*, I awoke one morning realizing that I had just dreamt in Hebrew. I was overwhelmed with joy that I had so quickly integrated the language into my psyche. But, there's always a "but", a few weeks later, Terry and I had a heart-to-heart. We seemed to be drifting apart, not communicating well, not sharing as we always had.

Suddenly, it hit us! For weeks, we had restricted our conversations at home to Hebrew in an effort to create a Hebrew-speaking environment and accelerate our language fluency. As a result, we stopped sharing our innermost feelings because we lacked the vocabulary to do so. We quickly made some language adjustments that preserved both our marriage and our Hebrew!

22. WHAT DO WE LEARN FROM THIS?

In rabbinic literature, the rabbis frequently ask the question: so what do we learn from this teaching or experience?

A Nourishing Community

First, we learn something about youth groups, Jewish summer camp, and peers who unite in common cause. Not only do they sharpen our skills and build our confidence, they also lay the foundation for interests, values, and family life that can sustain us for a lifetime.

Without Young Judaea, my formative years would have lacked the richness of close friendships, the confidence that grows from leadership, and my passionate love for the State of Israel.

Community is central to a rich Jewish experience. Without community, there are no synagogues, JCCs, rabbis, cantors, and teachers. With it, we embrace an extended Jewish family that in turn can embrace us with its many blessings. It's beneficial to our Jewish souls to live in a community with a critical mass of fellow Jews.

Immersion

Second, we learn that immersion can be magical. When we are intensely involved in a cause or activity, that concentration can transform our lives. For me, immersion has occurred only a handful of times, but when it did, it was amazing. Hebrew *ulpan* in Jerusalem packed a wallop. While we dealt with the marital hiccup that arose from speaking only Hebrew, we bought tomatoes in the local market, searched for a gasoline funnel for our motor scooter at a Beersheva hardware store, and delivered a sermon at an Israeli synagogue in the vernacular. That immersion year raised my comfort level with Hebrew to new heights--far more than if I had remained in Cincinnati for my fourth year (of five) of rabbinic studies. It confirmed that our decision had been correct.

Then there was that week-long music intensive at Peabody Institute in Baltimore that gifted Terry and me a love of a half-dozen works of classical music. To this day, every time I hear them, they move me to ecstasy. After Peabody, Mahler's Fifth and Beethoven's Seventh were never the same.

Another immersion was Marriage Encounter. After 25 years of marriage, we began to feel, as many couples do, that we had settled into a groove that was comfortable, but lacked rich communication and fresh renewal. When friends shared their positive experience at Marriage Encounter, we sprang for it.

Over several days, Terry and I explored new ways to communicate with greater honestly and regularity. We returned home with prescriptions for daily journaling and set times for couples' communication. (We delicately informed our children: "This is Mom and Dad's time. Please make yourselves scarce.") Like many immersive experiences, Marriage Encounter found its way inside our souls. Decades later, some of those insights still inform how we relate to each other, such as being able to recognize when communication has broken down and devoting more time to deeper interaction.

Friends report transformative experiences from other immersive programs such as Outward Bound (a skill-building intensive in the wilderness), culinary immersion in Italy, or weeks working an organic farm. Terry and I also discovered new sides of ourselves at Esalen Institute, Big Sur, California. There a playful spirit combined with bodywork and intellectual curiosity opened our eyes to novel ways of relating to nature and our own bodies. Rolling down a grassy knoll, mostly naked, was a moment of amazement that still sticks with me (pun intended).

Immersion does not require trips to exotic lands or costly programs. We immerse ourselves when we spend an entire night with a homeless family at a church or synagogue shelter or when we take care of a six-year old grandchild 24/7 while parents are away or when we intensively mentor a young student. Whatever form it takes, immersion breaks down barriers, opens new vistas, and blesses us with rewards that last a lifetime.

Timing

Third, timing helps. Because many of those experiences occurred when we were primed for personal growth, they made a lifetime of difference.

Some opportunities come only once in a lifetime: a partner who is just right, a unique business or professional opportunity, or a chance to study or work in another land. But many options are not one-off moments, such as learning a new skill or diving into a project or organization that helps to repair the world. They will reappear and, if we let one of those pass, we can revisit it at a later time. It is helpful to recognize which is which and to act accordingly.

My Best Friend

It was due to timing, good fortune, and something much more that I met Terry in the summer of 1953 when we were both counselors at Camp Blue Star, Hendersonville, NC. The "more" was that Blue Star was a camp that attracted members of Jewish youth groups, AZA, BBG, and Young Judaea, particularly from the Southeast where we grew up. That meant that most campers and staff shared much in common, like Zionism, Jewish community involvement, Jewish learning, religious traditions, and the distinctive culture of Southern Jewish life in cities like New Orleans, Birmingham, Atlanta, Jacksonville and Miami.

Timing was crucial. At the end of that summer, Terry would commence freshman year at Wellesley College near Boston and I would be a junior just 125 miles south in New Haven. When I learned that we were born just seven days apart and would both be studying in New England, I suspected that the stars were aligned for this match.

At this writing, after 67 years of marriage, most of what drew us to one another still does: similar family backgrounds, physical attraction, love of Israel and the Hebrew language, nature, hiking, exercise, intellectual pursuits, and the arts. What we share has deepened, especially classical music, jazz, great museums, swimming, travel, and...well, just guess. Bowing to age, sailing and downhill skiing have dropped off our list.

But one thing stands out as unchanging: Terry is my best friend and she says, well, most of the time, that I am hers. My best friend has been my best critic. She edits my sermons, reminds me that family comes first, and tells me to rev it back when my ego goes into overdrive.

We all need someone who will tell us the honest truth, even if it hurts. Who is your "truth teller?" Who will grab you by the collar and tell you lovingly, but firmly, that your ego is out of control or that your priorities are screwed up? Who informs you that you're not as important as you think you are, or that you're not taking good care of yourself?

If you do not have a "truth teller," get yourself one in the next seven days.

I admire Terry's affection and healthy guidance for our children when they were young (sneakers in snow never hurt a kid), her non-judgmental support, her love for our seven grandchildren, her seven-year pursuit of her PhD in English Literature, her excellence as a university instructor, her initiative in creating a 20-year newsletter business, her classy style, and her swim stroke.

She is cool under fire and does not let physical ailments rattle her. "Surgery? Doesn't worry me," she insists, "I'll just go to sleep and wake up. Nothing to it." No wonder she is my best friend, ten times over.

23. THE BLESSING OF A JEWISH STATE

Israel is not perfect. What sovereign state is? Its political system is dysfunctional (five national elections in three years!). The ultra-Orthodox drain the nation's resources as they birth generations of children who, with little or no secular education, are unemployable and destined to live in poverty. Resolution of the Israeli-Palestinian conflict remains remote. And Reform and Conservative Jews are still treated as second-class.

Israel was born into a dangerous neighborhood. In 1947, Richard Crossman, a British political leader who was not Jewish, told an anti-Zionist Baltimore rabbi that "the Jewish community cannot escape from the nationalism of the world it lives in. As a result, the Jewish State will be established in the worst possible way—by Jewish force" (Jorge Garcia Granados, *The Birth of Israel: The Drama As I Saw it.* New York, Knopf, 1948. pp. 43-44).

I hate war. I cringe at the slaughter of tens of millions in modern day conflicts. I cherish the teaching of Hillel: "Be of the disciples of Aaron, loving peace and pursuing peace" (*Ethics of the Fathers*, 1.12). Peace is one of Judaism's highest values. The rabbis taught "whoever establishes peace between two human beings, between husband and wife, between two cities, two nations, two families or two governments, no harm should come to that individual" *Mechilta Bachodesh*, 12).

And yet, we Jews must defend ourselves. For the first time in two millennia, the Jewish people exercises sovereign control over its own destiny. With sovereignty comes the responsibility of self-defense. In an ideal world, there would be no need for a "Jewish army." But Israelis face existential threats. That's why I shall be forever grateful for the IDF, the Israel Defense Force, which is an indispensible component of modern Jewish life.

At the same time, Israel needs to address the moral issues that flow from its occupation of the West Bank for more than half century. While AIPAC (American Israel Public Affairs Committee) has contributed mightily to Israel's security, today J Street also deserves our robust support because it addresses the moral issue of occupation, focuses on resolving the Israeli-Palestinian conflict, and pushes for a two-state solution. Israel must cease to expand West Bank settlements and must control extremists who beat Palestinians and burn their homes. When Israel becomes a beacon of moral values, it becomes not weaker, but stronger. Hundreds of former IDF commanders confirm that Israel can take steps toward a two-state solution without sacrificing national security. As American Jews who want Israel to remain democratic, Jewish, and secure, we need to advocate for this goal.

After *Kristallnacht*, the Night of Broken Glass, on November 9-10, 1938, Jews throughout Europe sought to flee fascism, but most nations slammed their borders shut. That included the United Kingdom that governed Palestine under a post-World War I mandate, and the United States where immigration was sharply limited by an isolationist State Department and well-placed xenophobes.

When Israel was established in 1948, the Law of Return guaranteed that any Jew on the planet could apply for citizenship. Had Israel existed 1933-45, millions who were murdered might have lived. Once established, Israel embraced the survivors, offered renewal and hope, and put Jewish values to work, building a just and compassionate society. Jews poured in from Arab lands, Iraq, Yemen, Libya, Syria and Tunisia, and later more than one million from the former Soviet Union and 150,000 from Ethiopia.

In 1987, my close friend, Rabbi Eric Yoffie, then Director of ARZA (Association of Reform Zionists of America) thought the time was right to create in Israel a version of the Religious Action Center of

Reform Judaism in Washington which has, since its founding in 1961, contributed so much to our nation's moral fabric. As president of ARZA, I partnered with Eric to help found the Israel Religious Action Center (IRAC) which today is the pre-eminent agency working for civil and human rights in Israel.

IRAC's creation was not a "walk in the park." Although we faced opposition from entrenched interests, we had the support of our Israeli colleagues and of Rabbi Alexander Schindler, the brilliantly intuitive leader of Reform Judaism.

Led for many years by the indomitable Anat Hoffman, IRAC fights every day for equal status for Reform and Conservative rabbis and synagogues, for gender, racial, and LGBTQ equality, and for the rights of converts and immigrants.

In Israel, we walk with our Biblical ancestors, with Jacob and Rebecca, Isaiah and Amos, David and Solomon. In Israel, we compose poetry, dance, and sing to the rhythm of their footsteps. In Israel, we celebrate Jewish holidays on the soil where those festivals originated. In Israel, we speak the sacred Hebrew language that sprang back to life a century ago. In Israel, breakthroughs in medicine and technology are improving the lives of people throughout the globe.

The day the State of Israel declared its Independence, my Jewish pride swelled. I thank God every day that I am blessed to live my life at this time when the Jewish people can be creative and free in the Promised Land. I hope you too can experience that blessing.

24. HOLDING ON TO JOY

I like to hold on to joy. Call it nostalgia, innocence, or whatever you wish. It makes me smile. Sometimes I go to sleep reenacting in my mind an exciting NY Mets win or---a night dancing at the White House.

It was March 26, 1979 when Terry and I found ourselves at the White House having dinner with President Jimmy and Roslyn Carter, President Anwar and Jehan Sadat of Egypt, Prime Minister Menachem and Aliza Begin of Israel and a few others. Actually, about a thousand others, celebrating the signing of the Israeli-Egyptian peace treaty. (Full disclosure: my cousin, Robert Lipshutz, was Carter's White House Counsel.)

What a joy to spend nearly seven unrushed hours at 1600 Pennsylvania Avenue celebrating the first peace agreement between Israel and any Arab state. Historians do not rank President Carter high among modern day occupants of the Oval Office. But he deserves high marks because the Israeli-Egyptian treaty, cold though it is, was Israel's first pact with any Arab state. It neutralized the largest and strongest military force in the Arab world. It has not only held firm for more than four decades, but Jordan signed peace accords 15 years later and now a half dozen more Arab states have followed suit. The 2020 Abraham Accords with the United Arab Emirates and others would not have been possible without peace with Egypt.

The joy of that evening did not remain untarnished. It rarely does. Sadat was assassinated 30 months later by Muslim extremists. But on that night, Itzhak Perlman and Pinchas Zukerman played, Leontyne Price sang, and the Kroloffs danced.

Oh, did we dance! About 30 minutes before midnight, we found ourselves at the entrance hall of the White House where the Marine Corps band played on. We seized the opportunity, grasped one another in joy, and danced our feet off until one a.m. At that point, we voluntarily approached the open door of the portico and slowly--very, very slowly--made our way down the iconic driveway. There wasn't a soul in our sight. No secret service, no uniformed officers, no official cars, just a plain ole' rabbi and his sweetheart wife. We knew this would never happen again. So we took our sweet time of it. We stretched what is normally a 60 second stroll, into a 10 minute crawl, one miniscule step after another, until we passed the security gate, waved through by the lone guard who offered an early morning tip of his hat. It is known as the "people's house." That night we certainly felt as though we owned a piece of it. And ever since.

I often relive that night when I explore pathways to peace in the Middle East, or when I seek common ground with people whose politics, religion, or ethnicity differ from mine, or...when I dance with Terry.

During the Covid19 pandemic, Terry and I were having dinner outside, at one of our favorite restaurants on West 68th Street in Manhattan. A saxophone player regaled the diners with tunes we love. As we rose to leave, we instinctively grabbed each other and started to dance the swing on the pavement. Patrons clapped, one took a video, and once again we frolicked our way home.

What moments of joy have you experienced and held on to? What have those moments meant to you and in what ways do they nourish you years later?

Perhaps it was the birth of a child or grandchild that opened up a new world. Or a family trip that you revisit in your mind over and over? Maybe it was a walk along a stream in woods whose solemnity brings you *sh'leimut* (peacefulness) years later. Possibly a Broadway musical whose tunes you still sing? Or a romantic moment that years later still holds for you the joy of bonding with your lover. Could it be a sermon or Bible lesson that opened your eyes to the Eternal? Some of us hold on, for a lifetime, to words of encouragement from a parent or grandparent, mentor, pastor, or teacher, counselor or friend. Many years may have passed, but they continue to guide and sustain us.

Think about the cherished moments that still resonate within you.

Do they empower you?
Do they give you hope?
Do they offer a pathway out of darkness?
Do they remind you of the beauty of life?
Or do they simply give you a warm, cuddly feeling?

Remember what Rabbi Heschel taught us: even fleeting moments can be transcendent and transformative. Hold on to them. Give them new life. Let them take you to the next step forward.

Beer and Insights in Bergen, Norway

You never know when or where your eyes will open to amazement. In 2018, Terry and I enjoyed a beer and the vista of historic Scandinavian architecture on a brilliantly sunny day at a dockside restaurant in Bergen, Norway, a charming city 427 miles from the Arctic Circle.

Hundreds of young people were luxuriating at nearby tables, One of them--a young 30ish woman--leaned over to inquire where we were from, at which point we launched into an eye opening conversation about the priorities in our lives. She explained how satisfying her life was in Norway, a country with not many poor people and few mega-rich. "Economically, most of us live in a narrow range," she observed, "grateful for universal health care, free education through a master's degree, and 70% of income guaranteed at retirement. We pay a lot of taxes, but we get just about everything we need." Norwegians hope to acquire a cabin by the water. But aside from that, their needs are mostly satisfied.

Of course, Norway is blessed with abundant offshore oil (discovered in 1969) that fuels its quality of life. Its small population is homogeneous, minimizing strife. But irrespective of those factors, the nation's values yield a sense of *shalom*. The Norwegians we met seem to be at peace with themselves and the world about them, in sync with nature, and grateful for their blessings. Our new friend then excused herself because she and her buddies were about to take a five-minute walk to attend a concert of world-class entertainers who regularly visit Bergen. Another blessing!

I have held on to that conversation for the life lessons that it offers and the *sh'leimut* (peacefulness) that it conveys.

The Psalmist reminds us:

> Teach us to count our days so that our hearts may grow in wisdom (Ps. 90:12).

What conversations have you had in recent months or years that offered you a new perspective, a different and helpful way to count your days and reflect on the purpose of your life?

25. DISCOVERING WISE HEARTS

I hope that you have been blessed with friends and family with wise hearts, who live their lives with sublime values and who put those values to work to make the world a better place.

My friend, Rabbi Bob Samuels, was a wise heart. He transformed the Leo Baeck School in Haifa, Israel (grades 1-6) into a premier educational center with a vast campus serving 2400 children, K-12. Embedded within Leo Baeck are a Reform synagogue community, programs for Ethiopian Jews, and an Arab-Jewish initiative. Bob devoted his life to lifting up the hungry, educating the young, and bringing together people who were hesitant to sit in the same room with one another.

My college roommate, Bill Piper, also has a wise heart. Bill has carried forward his family's historic seven-generation-legacy by giving back to his native city, Flint, Michigan. His generous philanthropy, church stewardship, and communal leadership inspire me everyday. He and I, separated by 660 miles, enjoy a friendship that is closer than ever.

Another wise heart is Warren Eisenberg, discussed earlier. Beyond our 20-year partnership with the "I Have A Dream" program, I resonate to his support of Israeli peace initiatives, Arab-Jewish cooperation, social justice in Israel, and summer programs for low-income seniors. But most of all, I delight in the fact that Warren, like my college buddy, Bill, pursues his good works with humility.

Jewish tradition teaches that humility is one of the most important human qualities. The Torah describes Moses, the greatest leader in Jewish history, as "a very humble man, more so than any other man on earth" (Numbers 12.3). The prophet Micah calls on us to "walk humbly with God" (Micah 6.8)

When the Talmudic schools--Bet Hillel and Bet Shammai--disagreed, Hillel's opinion usually, but not always, prevailed. However, the dissent of the School of Shammai is preserved in our literature and is often studied for a new perspective. There is a deep sense of humility in rabbinic tradition, recognizing that what appears to be correct today must always be subject to reexamination. Today's minority opinion could become tomorrow's majority.

Most rabbis don't do well with humility. Preaching to a thousand people on the Holydays feeds the ego. So do the kudos we receive for simply doing our job at weddings and funerals. Some of us fear that if we are too laid back, it will be interpreted as weakness and that we'll be taken advantage of.

A wise heart is a generous heart that understands where we have come from and where we will eventually go. A wise heart tries to live by the teaching of Rabbi Bunim of P'shiska: everyone should carry two slips of paper, one in each pocket. The first states, "I am but dust and ashes." The second declares, "I am created in the image of God." The wise heart balances both.

Who are the people in your orbit who have a wise heart? Who has achieved that precious balance between self-confidence and humility?

Whom do you admire? What are the qualities that you appreciate in them? What impact do they have on you?

If there are no wise hearts in your orbit, where can you start to look for them?

26. PREPARE TO BE SURPRISED

Riding the Emotional Roller-Coaster

I had been ordained barely 16 months, embarking on my second year as assistant rabbi of Temple Israel, Boston. It was one o'clock on a bright Sunday as I knocked on the door of a stately home in Chestnut Hill where I was to perform an afternoon wedding. The father of the bride greeted me at the entrance, took one look at me, and asked, "Rabbi, what's wrong? You've come to a happy occasion and you look so sad!"

I quickly realized what was going on and explained: "I've just come from a funeral at the Temple and then the cemetery where I buried a 14-year-old boy. Last year, I officiated at his bar mitzvah and three days ago he was running to catch the MTA, slipped on ice, and was caught under the wheels of the train. I realize now that emotionally I am still at the funeral."

I excused myself, headed to the restroom where I splashed cold water on my face, pulled myself together, and plunged into my role as joyful officiant, front-and-center.

The life of a clergyperson who serves a congregation is an emotional roller coaster. In the course of eight hours, we can be on the floor singing with four year olds, standing by the bedside of a terminally ill patient, comforting a grieving family, sitting in our study counseling a devastated wife facing divorce and, as evening arrives, trying to teach a bunch of 16-year-olds who want to be somewhere else. It's a nearly impossible juggling act to be emotionally involved and cool as a cucumber!

Years ago, I was officiating at the wedding of a young woman who had grown up at Temple Emanu-El. In the middle of the ceremony, the groom made eye contact with a friend seated on the aisle. In what seemed like a nanosecond, the friend jumped from his seat, slipped behind the *chuppah*, flipped a switch, and suddenly hidden speakers blasted forth the loudest rock and roll I had ever heard.

The bride froze, and so did I. Within seconds, she turned to the groom and with measured anger said, "If you don't turn that off this second, I will walk out of here right now." He followed her order. I brushed off my rage, took three deep breaths, and proceeded as if nothing had happened. "You're in charge," I said to myself, "get to the end of this and exit out of here as quickly as possible." Rage suppressed. Cool head prevailed.

The next day, bright and early, the bride's parents, caring people whom I respected, called to apologize, explaining that the groom, a sportscaster, thought that blasting his bride's favorite song in the middle of the ceremony would be a great gift to her.

At another wedding, outdoors in the Berkshires, I drove onto an open field with 200 guests gathered in 90 degree temperature, only to be told that the groom had gotten cold feet and walked into the woods. "Rabbi, you're the only one who can do anything about this. He went....that way."

Surprises, emotional roller coasters, being present at tumultuous times, and teaching restless teens—I wouldn't trade them for all the stock options in the world. Like the vast majority of my colleagues, I feel privileged to be invited into the most personal, the most challenging, and the most joyful moments in the lives of my congregants. I feel honored to teach Torah, Commentaries, Heschel, Buber, Zionism, and Jewish values to those who are searching and seeking. And what a privilege it is—as many of my friends in medicine, dentistry, law, education, counseling, and business can attest—to teach the next generation, confidant that they will do better than we.

27. MARRIAGE NEVER STAYS THE SAME

Much attention is devoted to the wedding ceremony. The New York Times reserves half a section every Sunday to the subject. But what's most important is what follows the ceremony. My advice to couples during pre-marital counseling is: "Don't be surprised when you hit some bumps in the road. It happens to every couple. And don't wait too long to seek help when you cannot resolve issues by yourself."

Once I completed professional training, I provided marital and family therapy to hundreds of people, some synagogue members and some clients. Marriages never stay the same. They either get much better or much worse. We either grow closer or further apart.

It's important to take our marital temperature regularly. We human beings are not static creatures. We grow; we change; we develop new interests and new needs. Many a spouse wakes up one morning and says silently, "I don't recognize my partner anymore. She/he/they is so different from the person I married 25 years ago." Or "I barely recognize myself. I'm interested in things I never even thought about when we married. We have so little in common now."

The changes pile up and--when we're fortunate-- those changes are precisely the stuff that can make our lives together amazing. (Remember Rabbi Heschel who urges us to be amazed.) But those very same changes can be a minefield if we don't explore them with our spouse and navigate them in ways that draw us closer, rather than push us further apart.

Here's an example: When Naomi (not her real name) married at age 23, she lacked self-confidence and depended on her father for guidance. She was attracted to her husband (let's call him Ned) because he exuded strength, making it easy for her to shift her dependence from Dad to Ned.

After four children and a Masters in Business Administration, Naomi began to acquire a name for herself in the corporate world. By then, she became aware of what had been evolving over many years: her dependence on Ned had diminished and her self-reliance had soared. But Naomi and Ned had been so busy with children, work, and physical fitness that they rarely thought about--let alone spoke about—what was happening to their marriage.

Had they taken their "marriage temperature" regularly, they might have recognized that the changes that were occurring to them individually were slowly, almost imperceptibly, eroding their marriage. Early recognition of these changes might have led to midcourse corrections. No guarantees. But without recognition and intervention, the chances for the marriage to endure were slim.

On our 67th wedding anniversary, Terry and I decided to add a new element to our special day. In addition to congratulations offered on classical WQXR-FM, a hike in the Watchung mountains, and a fine dinner, we shouted out (literally) what we loved about each other. I took the morning slot and Terry the afternoon. Spontaneously and with a sense of utter delight, we cried out what we adored: your optimism and patience, your swim stroke and love of nature, your willingness to watch the NY Mets with me and your affection for horses, ice cream, Shakespeare, and flowers. Because it was novel, authentic, and liberating, this playful exercise brought us closer together

The Covid-19 pandemic and the disruptions that flow from it have raised anxiety levels worldwide. Four in 10 adults nationwide reported symptoms of anxiety or depressive disorder since the start of the pandemic, exacerbating marital stress (*New York Times*, Jan. 20, 2022, p. ST 11).

But even in more normal times, there is hardly a marriage on earth that does not require periodic evaluation, midcourse correction, and liberating, playful experiences. When those steps are taken, the odds rise that a couple will travel into the sunset with a love that--having been frequently renewed--will flourish.

Intermarriage

What about intermarriage between Jews and non-Jews? For most of my rabbinate, I did not officiate at these weddings. I thought, as did nearly all of my Reform colleagues at that time, that by not officiating I could discourage such unions. And there was likely some truth to this in the 1960s and 70s. But in the decades to follow, socialization between Jews and non-Jews--on college campuses, at the workplace, at bars and ball fields--became the norm and by 2021 Jews were marrying non-Jews at rates exceeding 70 percent.

IN 1978, Rabbi Alexander Schindler, urged American Jews to engage in "Outreach" which meant actively welcoming non-Jewish spouses and the children of mixed marriages into our synagogue communities. His initiative, which was met with reservations, eventually has become the *modus operandi* of nearly every non-Orthodox synagogue in America. Marriage between Jews and non-Jews is not new. Moses married Zipporah who was a Midianite. In the Book of Ruth we learn that Boaz married Ruth, a Moabite. Ruth is considered the first Jew-by-Choice and, according to tradition, King David is her descendent.

In 2008, I chaired the CCAR Task Force on the Challenge of Intermarriage for the Reform Rabbi. Halfway through our three years of deliberations, it became clear to many of us on the taskforce that, by not officiating, we were unable to be with our students and congregants at this important moment in their lives. It also meant that sometimes pre-marital discussions with a skilled rabbi, important for the couple's future, were either abbreviated or non-existent. This lack of rabbinic presence often resulted in their alienation from rabbis and synagogues and a growing tension between rabbis and congregants.

At the same time, our taskforce learned about creative rabbinic initiatives that resulted in these couples being warmly welcomed and engaged in synagogue life. In other words, Rabbi Schindler's Outreach was working. This was also substantiated by surveys indicating that higher percentages of intermarried couples were choosing to join synagogues and raise their children as Jews.

The 2013 Pew study of American Jewish life revealed that 33 percent of intermarried couples were rearing their offspring as Jews. (You need at least 50% to break even.) I was astounded that by the time of the 2021 Pew study, that number had climbed to 57%. Mathematically, that could mean that--as a result of children in inter-married homes growing up Jewish--our numbers could be increasing. Add to the equation the fact that families with just one Jewish spouse are frequently active, committed members of liberal synagogues. Since the Jewish intermarriage rate hovers around 72%, with no reason to expect it to drop, these are encouraging developments.

I have great respect for those of my colleagues who do not officiate at inter-faith marriages and who, at the same time, are engaged in counseling and supporting those couples. Theirs is a principled position and those rabbis work hard at sustaining the Jewish future. At the same time, I believe that those rabbis who do now officiate should do everything they can to encourage inter-married couples to establish a Jewish home and, should they bear children, to raise those children as Jewish girls and boys. Our synagogues have a responsibility to provide quality Jewish education and to support those families as they navigate their unique challenges.

28. WHY BASEBALL? WHY THE METS?

I've been a fan of baseball since I was about six, growing up on Chicago's Southside and following the White Sox like they were family. I fell asleep at night furtively glued to Sox' games on my homemade single-cell radio. That tradition continued when we moved south, where my allegiance shifted to our hometown Atlanta Crackers of Class AA Southern Association. In Cincinnati and Boston, I was too preoccupied to pay much attention to the Reds and the Red Sox. But once we hit the New York region, it was all about the Mets.

Why baseball and why the Mets who have won exactly two World Series titles in 60 years? Baseball attracted kids like me because we could identify with the players. Unlike football, players needn't be the biggest and strongest. Unlike basketball, they aren't the tallest. Unlike tennis, they aren't the smoothest. You don't need 100 yards of turf or even a basketball hoop hung 10 feet high. A stick and rock sometimes make do. Accessible is the name of the game.

Dads and sons (and Moms and daughters) bond over baseball. My Dad and I talked endlessly about Hank Greenberg of the Detroit Tigers, the first Jewish ballplayer to enter Baseball's Hall of Fame. Dad's Jewish pride became mine as he regaled me with the story of Greenberg's decision, during the heated 1934 pennant race, to sit out a game because it occurred on Yom Kippur.

Edgar Guest, one of my father's favorite columnists, captured what Greenberg's momentous decision meant in his poem, "The Jewish Casey."

"The Irish didn't like it when they heard of Greenberg's fame,
For they thought a good first baseman should possess an Irish name;
And the Murphys and Mulrooneys said they never dreamed they'd see,
A Jewish boy from Bronxville out where Casey used to be.
In the early days of April not a Dugan tipped his hat,
Or prayed to see a double when Hank Greenberg came to bat.

In July the Irish wondered where he'd ever learned to play.
'He makes me think of Casey!' Old Man Murphy dared to say;
And with fifty-seven doubles and a score of homers made,
 The respect they had for Greenberg was being openly displayed.

But on the Jewish New Year when Hank Greenberg came to bat,
And made two home runs off Pitcher Rhodes—they cheered like mad for that.
Came Yom Kippur—holy fast day worldwide over to the Jew,
And Hank Greenberg to his teaching and the old tradition true,

Spent the day among his people and he didn't come to play.
Said Murphy to Mulrooney, 'We shall lose the game today!

We shall miss him on the infield and shall miss him at
the bat,
But he's true to his religion—and I honor him for
that!'"

For most Jewish kids of my generation who experienced anti-Semitism growing up, Greenberg was our answer. If a kid wasn't sure why the High Holydays were so important, Greenberg clarified that. And as Murphy said to Mulrooney, "I honor him for that," so Jewish kids were honored by the story our Dads told us about Greenberg. We were honored also when Sandy Koufax skipped the first game of the World Series on Yom Kippur. That was six years after my father died, but I knew he would have admired Koufax as much as he adored Greenberg.

Baseball is generational. During the Covid pandemic, four Kroloffs wove a nearly daily email thread around our beloved Mets. That thread snaked across two continents and spanned three-and-a-half generations. During the 2021 season, we posted between innings, celebrating the Mets' 91 days in first place in the National League East. We comforted one another when our All-Star pitcher, Jacob deGrom (aka "Uncle Jake"), went on the Injured List and we wondered when Francisco Lindor (10 seasons/$341M) would recover from his batting doldrums. At season's end, emails flew between us celebrating the Mets' acquisition of Max Scherzer, one of the game's top hurlers.

There are not many traditions that can firmly bond four family members whose ages span more than 70 years. Judaism, or whatever religion might anchor your family, can bind the generations. Judaism has provided a spiritual bond for us with our sons and daughter, Micah, Noah, Sarah, and their families.

But back to baseball. It's also philosophy of life.
You welcome a walk, but can't wait to get home.

Whatever you do, don't get caught off base.
You'd much rather be called safe than make an error.
Stay off the Injured List and avoid balking.
Greet each day as a new opportunity, even if you lost yesterday.
Better to be a Major player than a Minor one.
Trainers keep you limber and coaches straighten you out.
It takes a team.
The line between fair and foul is very thin.
It's the only place where stealing is legal.
No one is perfect (except for a few pitchers).
If you nail three out of ten, you're darn good.
And as Yogi Berra declared: "It ain't over 'till it's over."

Thanks to Branch Rickey, Jackie Robinson and Larry Doby, the only race that matters is the race to the bag. In the words of the Detroit Tigers (and one time Atlanta Crackers) sportscaster, Ernie Harwell, color is merely something that distinguishes one team's uniform from another.

But why the Mets? Geography had a say. When the Mets were born in 1962, we lived on Long Island, a short hop to Shea Stadium in Queens. Once again the hometown team was a draw.

But there is much more. We Jews identify with the oppressed and the Mets quickly qualified. In their first year, they lost 120 games, three out of every four. Pathetic underdogs. But the bleeding didn't stop. In 1963, the losses were 111. The next year they "improved" to 109 losses, then back to 112. At least they were consistent, last place outliers. One of baseball's attractions is that no matter what happens on a given day, you have a decent chance for a win the next day. Well, not so decent with our poverty-stricken Mets.

In 1969, lightning struck. The Miracle Mets turned the numbers upside down--not losing, but winning 100--and capturing the World Series from the highly-favored Baltimore Orioles in five games with the likes of Tom Seaver, Jerry Koosman, and Cleon Jones. Micah (age 9) and I sat behind the third base dugout at Baltimore's Memorial Stadium as our much maligned Mets squeaked out a 2-1 victory on a bright October Sunday. As we flew back that evening with our host and friend Herb Brody, founder of Pathmark Supermarkets, could this father and son ever imagine that our love affair with those rag-tag outliers from Queens would endure more than half a century later across the generations?

If you don't keep up with the times, you die. Baseball is learning that truth. Pitchers have become so dominant that they are mowing down the hitters with their fastballs. Too many strikeouts equals boring. Batters are stronger so home runs have mushroomed. Many homers = fewer balls in play = more boring. The games are too long and diversity has suffered. While 30% of major league players are Hispanic, only 7% are black.

So what are the takeaways?

Youthful indiscretions aren't all bad.
Jewish pride flows from many sources.
An activity that binds the generations is priceless.
Don't give up on the underdog.
Keep the faith.
To remain relevant, keep up with the times.
Miracles do happen!

29. GROWING INTO THE SUNSET

Aging is most often associated with loss: loss of friends, loss of strength, diminished visual acuity and impaired cognition. The list goes on until the weight of aging seems overwhelming.

There is, however, another way to view aging. Lean back with me to the 12th century and consider the perspective of the Chinese poet, Lu Yu:

Old man pushing seventy,
In truth he acts like a little boy,
Whooping with delight when he spies some mountain fruits,
Laughing with joy, tagging after village mummers;
With the others having fun stacking tiles to make a pagoda,
Standing alone staring at his image in the jardinière pool.
Tucked under his arm, a battered book to read,
Just like the time he first set out to school.

I find myself sometimes "whooping with delight," as Terry and I enjoy a cartoon from an old *New Yorker* magazine by Chas Adams (he grew up in Westfield), or as we take in a raucous episode of "The Marvelous Mrs. Maisel" or "Only Murders in the Building." Sometimes I will tag after an interesting gaggle in Central Park as I revel in their antics or I'll follow a silver jet as it ascends from Newark Liberty streaking through pure blue sky, destination unknown.

There are times when I feel like Lu Yu's little boy first setting out to school. Is it possible that I might learn something new today like that little boy I once was? Or that I might delight in a brand new experience, such as the moment when I hear just four notes of a classical composition and it sounds like an old friend. Those are the times when I feel like the first grader who, when his teacher asks a question, raises his hand in a second, proudly blurting out a correct answer.

It may seem contradictory (life is replete with contradictions) but, at the same time, I welcome the peace that comes with old age. Consider Czeslaw Milosz's observation in *Late Ripeness*:

"Not soon, as late as the approach of my ninetieth year, I felt a door opening in me and I entered the clarity of early morning."

Joy comes wrapped in many packages. In each decade of life, the wrapping and the contents look different. Pandemics distort the packaging, but clarify the contents.

Cherish the joys in every day because eventually those parcels will be marked "return to sender."

ACKNOWLEDGEMENTS

I am grateful to Arielle Kroloff, Sheila Lombardi, Rabbi Sally Priesand, Fr. Anthony Randazzo, Rabbi Laurie Rice, and S.J. Tagliareni for their close reading of the manuscript. My friend, Rabbi Joel Soffin, was an initial source of inspiration for this book. The cover is the work of the superbly talented artist, Paul Jennis. I am filled with gratitude to Paul who shares my admiration of Martin Buber.

My appreciation runs deep for the members of Temple Emanu-El who have encouraged me in my rabbinic odyssey, permitted me to share in their life's journey, and have forgiven me when I came up short. We have been blessed with an extraordinary number of devoted congregants and enlightened leaders and to each of them I shall be forever grateful. Contributions to the Rabbi Kroloff Fund for Jewish Learning have assisted in the distribution of this book.

As they frequently do when I am involved in a personal project, our sons, Micah and Noah Kroloff, our daughter, Sarah Kroloff Segal, and their spouses, Donna Etkins, Roger Segal, and Claudia Green offered helpful critique and encouragement. They and their families bring us blessing every day. Above all, my gratitude overflows to my wife, Terry, for her literary insights, her optimistic perspective on life, and her unequivocal love and support that have sustained me and blessed me since we first met in Hendersonville, North Carolina at age18.

Charles A. Kroloff

Westfield, New Jersey
July 15, 2022

ABOUT THE AUTHOR

Rabbi Charles A. Kroloff was spiritual leader of Temple Emanu-El, Westfield, New Jersey, for 36 years and is past president of the Central Conference of American Rabbis. A graduate of Yale University, he was ordained at Hebrew Union College-Jewish Institute of Religion where he taught rabbinic students for three decades. His previous books include When Elijah Knocks: A Religious Response to Homelessness and 54 Ways You Can Help the Homeless. Rabbi Kroloff and his wife, Dr. Terry Kroloff, are the parents of three children who, with their spouses, have blessed them with seven grandchildren.

CPSIA information can be obtained
at www.ICGtesting.com
Printed in the USA
BVHW041547111022
649147BV00005B/722